Newman's Own

Cookbook

Newman's Own

Cookbook

Paul Newman
and A. E. Hotchner

with the culinary and editorial assistance of
Lisa Stalvey and Evie Righter

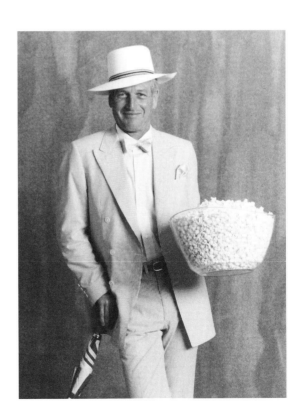

Ebury Press
London

First published in the United Kingdom in 1999 by Ebury Press

1 3 5 7 9 10 8 6 4 2

Text © Hole in the Wall Gang Fund Inc. 1999

This edition first published in the United Kingdom in 1999 by Ebury Press
Random House, 20 Vauxhall Bridge Road, London SW1V 2SA

Random House Australia (Pty) Limited
20 Alfred Street, Milsons Point, Sydney,
New South Wales 2061, Australia

Random House New Zealand Limited
18 Poland Road, Glenfield, Auckland 10, New Zealand

Random House South Africa (Pty) Limited
Endulini, 5a Jubilee Road, Parktown 2193, South Africa

Random House UK Limited Reg. No. 954009

A CIP catalogue record for this book is available from the British Library

ISBN 0 09 186926 9

Printed and bound in Great Britain by Butler and Tanner Ltd, Frome, Somerset

Designed by Richard Oriolo

Photos by Janet Durrans appear on pages 22, 42, 68, 72, 79,
113, 145, 158, 201, and 203

Acknowledgments

Newman and Hotchner cleverly overcame their limited culinary skills by enlisting the invaluable assistance of their editor, Sydny Miner, and Newman's Own food consultant Lisa Stalvey, who contributed her imaginative recipes. The authors are also indebted to food expert and writer Evie Righter.

This book is dedicated to our customers, whose loyalty makes it possible for us to help those who need help.

Contents

Preface My adult life has been spent in the family of women: my wife, Joanne; five daughters; my housekeeper, Caroline; and a succession of wirehaired terriers, all males who were immediately castrated upon arrival. No wonder I took to wearing an apron by way of disguise, lest I become a capon. What started out as a protective measure became, over time, a stunning discovery of culinary treasures.

These discoveries result from my ability to establish a relationship with the food I'm about to cook. Have you ever had a meaningful conversation with a fillet of cod? Or a dialogue with a slice of calves' liver?

When I'm about to do some serious cooking, I get ready by putting myself into a self-induced hypnotic trance, much in the same way the Shakirs trance themselves so that they can walk over hot coals and sleep comfortably on a bed of razor-sharp spikes.

Once I'm in my trance, I hold the fillet of cod in close proximity to my face, and I listen to it. The first sound I hear is that of a popping cork, then the faint sound of cows mooing, and finally the crackling sound of fire. The popping cork leads me to white wine, the moo-cows denote butter, and the roaring fire suggests black basil, all of which I use for my cod dish (page 104). Over the years I've had several conversations with cod, and although there may have been a few variations (a ticking clock obviously indicated thyme), for the most part the cod always had the same things to say to me.

My cooking method becomes more difficult when I cook at somebody else's house—a brisket of beef, say—because my host and hostess constantly interrupt my trance by offering me a Bloody Mary or a slice of local pâté. It's hard enough to get a brisket of beef to speak up without having to politely reject booze and hors d'œuvres in the process.

Many of the recipes in this book are the result of animated conversations with fish, fowl, fauna and flora. You may be a bit sceptical of my method—as have been many before you—but to all those snicklers, snipers, and sniders I can only say that after the plates, knives, forks, napkins and tablecloths were licked clean, nobody ever quarrelled with the mystical, magical results of this intimate relationship between the chef and his victuals.

—Paul Newman

Introduction

I have been asked many times how Paul Newman, who knows a great deal about acting but very little about business, and I, a writer who knows even less, became tycoons—and in the food business yet, as competitive and cutthroat an industry as you can find in Dun & Bradstreet.

The answer is: we did everything wrong. We did just the opposite of what the experts told us to do. Actually, we started with virtually no capital in the bank—a couple of bumbling amateurs trying to fish with no bait in a sea of sharks. It is one thing to want to put a bottle of salad dressing on supermarket shelves but quite another to get it there, and to that end Paul and I consulted a bevy of food experts. We met with the top people of a big marketing company; they advised us to invest a half-million dollars and test the product in 'key' shopping plazas all around the United States. 'We test-market for Campbell's, Libby, Heinz, and all the biggies,' they told us, 'and that's how all of them handle a new product.' Another big food executive told us that the salad dressing competition was so keen our only chance was to sell our bottles by mail order. And then there was the financial consultant, his desk covered with statistical charts and summaries, who informed us convincingly that we should be prepared to lose $1 million in the first year of operation.

We digested all this, and Newman spoke my mind: 'Hotch,' he said, 'I'll tell you what. Let's test-market it by inviting some of our friends to come over and sample it along with the dressings of all our competitors, using unmarked dishes. If we beat the others, then let's fly right in the teeth of the competition and try to get it on the supermarket shelves. To hell with mail order. And I think we should put up forty thousand dollars instead of a million—how about it?'

We shook on it and set up a corporation that we originally called Salad King, with Newman as president and me as vice-president and treasurer. Now, before I go any

Newman and Hotchner at work

further, I suppose I had better fill you in on how we got involved with salad dressing in the first place. As long as I can remember, Newman has been rejecting so-called house dressings and concocting his own mix. Captains, maître d's, and sometimes the restaurant owners themselves would scurry around to assemble Newman's ingredients. When we first ate at Elaine's, one of New York's 'in' restaurants, virtually all the waiters and Elaine herself gathered around as Paul blended and tasted the ingredients that had been brought to him from the kitchen.

I have watched this scene repeated in a Greek diner, at a wedding party, and in various restaurants from coast to coast. When his kids went off to school, they would ask him to fill a couple of bottles of the salad dressing for them to take along.

All well and good until that day when Paul came over one afternoon to watch a football game and said, 'I have a neat idea for Christmas presents. I'm going to give all my friends bottles of my salad dressing. They're always asking me for the recipe, so I'll fill up all the empty wine bottles I've been saving and play Santa Claus. Good idea, huh?'

'Great. They'll love it,' I said naively.

'When can we start?'

'Start what?'

'Making the dressing. I figure you and I can do it in an afternoon. How about tomorrow?'

As devious as Tom Sawyer, he is. It took us eight hours of steady labour to mix it, bottle it, cork it and wrap it. But Newman's friends were delighted, and it was a ritual Paul and I followed every Christmas after that, each year taking longer than the year before, as the list of requests for 'Newman's Own Salad Dressing' grew longer and longer.

But finally my sagging back cracked under the mounting pressure. It was the year that it took us three days of sweatshop labour down in Newman's cellar to turn out enough bottles to satisfy his list, by then three pages long. At the end of the third day, Paul stood in the centre of the cellar surrounded by all those filled bottles and suggested that we do an extra one hundred bottles and put them up for sale in local food stores.

'You can't stand the thought that on Christmas Day there will be people around here eating salad without your dressing on it, that it?'

He nodded. 'How can we be so selfish? Spread good cheer, I say. What's a few more days of bottling?'

I didn't tell him. Instead I said, 'It's against the law.'

'What is? There is absolutely nothing in my dressing that's illegal.'

'The Pure Food Law. You have to have certain certificates.'

'Okay, let's look into it.'

That was how it started, innocently enough, but over the next several months Newman was driven by his desire to market his dressing. Scarcely a day passed without Paul's calling from some unlikely place to discuss a newly discovered source for the perfect olive oil, the perfect red wine vinegar, or the perfect mustard that he constantly sought. He phoned me from racetracks in between races, from mobile dressing rooms while shooting *Absence of Malice* and *The Verdict*, and from airports on his way to make speeches on behalf of the nuclear freeze movement.

That's when I said, 'Listen, Paul, we've been friends for forty-odd years [some of them *really* odd], and I wonder why you're so fixed on marketing your dressing. I ask you, would Clark Gable sell salad dressing? Would Tyrone Power? Humphrey Bogart? Isn't it a little tacky?'

'It's all-natural,' Newman said, a touch of pique in his tone. 'Just look at the labels on all these other dressings—full of gums, preservatives, chemical additives. That's why. And there's something else.'

'What?'

'If we are successful—'

'Yes?'

'I'll tell you then.'

So we started operations by finding a modest marketing company in Port Washington, New York, to sell our product, an obscure bottler in Boston to bottle it, and with a total of $40,000 as the entire capital of Salad King, Inc., we set up our headquarters in a little office in Westport, Connecticut, that we furnished with Paul's poolside furniture; in fact, our desk still has a beach umbrella over it. We do not advertise (until this day we haven't spent a penny on advertising), but within a month after our first bottle of Newman's Own had reached the shelves, we had repaid the $40,000 and the orders were rolling in.

It was at the end of our first year of operation, poised by then to introduce a second product—Newman's Own Industrial Strength Marinara Sauce—that Paul said, 'We have made nine hundred and twenty thousand dollars in profit, and it's tacky for an actor and a writer to be making money in the food business. So let's give it all away to them what needs it.'

That was fifteen years ago, and in those fifteen years we have sold 216,262,680 bottles of Newman's Own oil and vinegar salad dressing; 149,531,280 jars of pasta sauce; 3,278,497,493 portions of popcorn; 37,142,909 jars of salsa; and 81,650,032 pints of lemonade, amounting to $710 million in gross sales. Our total profit from these products to date has been approximately $100 million, every penny of which has been given to deserving charities—a total of 6,088 contributions. We are told that we are the only corporation in the world that gives away all of its profits and starts with zero dollars in the bank on the first of each fiscal year.

So what started out as a lark has become, to our everlasting amazement, a virtual food empire. We have ten factories in the United States and our own trucking network. We are widely distributed in such faraway places as Australia, Japan, Greenland, Puerto Rico, Guam and England.

'In the beginning,' Paul has said, 'we were pretty bewildered, trying to decide which among the vast number of deserving charities we should give to. But by now we've developed a pretty good concept—concentrating on organizations for the very young and the very old. But these profits also give me a chance to repay those places that helped me when I needed them: Kenyon University, where I went to school and which whetted my appetite for the stage; Yale University drama school, which firmed my resolve to be an actor; the Neighborhood Playhouse and the Actors Studio in New York, where marvellous theatre people taught me and encouraged me and put me on the track to a career. It's a kick to be able to give these places solid grants of money so that they can help other young people as they helped me.

'Of course, most of our donations go to major charities, such as Sloan Kettering Cancer Research, Lahey Clinic, New York Foundling Hospital, Cystic Fibrosis, Society to Advance the Retarded, Harlem Restoration, and the American Foundation for AIDS Research, but the biggest kick Hotch and I get is when we can help little obscure organizations that couldn't generate the publicity to attract the attention of big donors.'

For example, in 1984 we received this letter written by Sister Carol Putnam, a Sacred Heart nun who ran the Hope Rural School in Indiantown, Florida. 'I am hurting desperately for help for a new bus. Ours does not pass inspection for the fall. A new bus costs $26,000. I have written to several sources and have gotten a "no" so far. A bus will last us ten years and we cannot pick up the children without one.'

We phoned Sister Carol and discovered that Hope Rural, which is a school for the children of migrant farmworkers, might have to go out of existence because its fourteen-year-old secondhand school bus had been condemned.

Prior to the founding of the Hope Rural School, the children had been denied any consistent schooling. They were prevented from attending regular classes by the wretched poverty that forced their farmworker families to travel constantly throughout the country in search of seasonal work. The youngsters often laboured in the fields alongside their parents, returning to central Florida every winter to harvest the state's citrus crops; when times got particularly hard, these families slept under bridges and in abandoned cars. Many of the children had never held a schoolbook or heard a nursery rhyme until the Hope Rural School, built by the migrant workers themselves, began a flexible term that allowed the children to attend classes during the picking season without having to enrol in a normal September-to-June school year.

'But when our school bus was condemned this past summer by the state authorities, my worst fears were realized,' Sister Carol told us. 'With no bus to transport these children from their homes miles away, the school would be worthless, and many of the children would return to their hopeless lives in the fields.'

Sister Carol said she had taken $1,000 that had been earmarked for teachers' salaries and put a down payment on a new school bus, hoping that somehow, some way, someone would donate money for the bus. The sisters at Hope Rural had written to foundations and called wealthy men and women from the nearby Palm Beach area, but the school could find no one willing to help. And then, the day before our phone call, as time and hope were running out, tragedy almost struck.

It was a blisteringly hot November afternoon, and the condemned school bus was making its way along back roads to bring a handful of students home for the day. As the bus approached the flashing lights of a railroad crossing, the driver applied the brakes, but the brakes wouldn't hold and the bus continued on toward the tracks. Warning whistles blared the approach of the Amtrack express from Tampa, but with no time to get the children out, the driver decided to put his foot down, charging across the tracks moments before the train swept by.

The very day that we spoke with Sister Carol, our cheque for the immediate delivery of a new bus to Hope Rural was on its way to the Blue Bird Bus Company.

In 1997, after thirteen years of hard use, the nuns of Hope Rural informed us that the bus had worn out, and we happily sent them a replacement.

We have a substantial Canadian market, and we annually donate all our Canadian profits to three charities there: the Hospital for Sick Children, the St. Boniface General Hospital Research Foundation, and the Famous People Players, a remarkable nonprofit group of black light puppeteers who have performed all over the world, most recently in China. Ten of the thirteen members of the troupe are mentally handicapped.

As we do with Canada, we also return to Australian and British charities (we have factories in both countries) the substantial profits that we realize from the sale of our products there and in every foreign country where we do business. At present we make donations to charities in Africa, Argentina, Australia, Bolivia, Bosnia, Brazil, Cambodia, Canada, Croatia, Czechoslovakia, Denmark, El Salvador, France, Germany,

Haiti, Hong Kong, Iceland, Ireland, Israel, Japan, Korea, New Zealand, Russia, Sweden, Switzerland, the United Kingdom and Vietnam.

Newman and I have always had a lively and inquisitive interest in food, as the recipes in this book will attest. We have recommended the use of our high-quality products, but certainly you can replace our stuff with other brands if you prefer. The recipes themselves come from three sources:

1. Some are our own favourites, invented by us, while others are contributions from family and friends.

2. Some are recipes that won the contest that we sponsor every year in conjunction with *Good Housekeeping* magazine. The contest awards cash prizes to the winners' designated charities. There are special contest categories for children and for professional food critics.

3. Some were concocted for us by a young chef named Lisa Stalvey, whom we met when Paul and I regularly dined at her restaurant in Santa Monica while Newman was filming his movie *Twilight*.

As for Newman's personal recipes, you will find that the dishes he cooks have his own characteristics—simple, straightforward, good quality, just enough seasoning to be exciting but not overwhelming, with an unexpected flair, a touch of the exotic. Even his hamburger. Really. Give it a try.

—A. E. HOTCHNER

It's our belief that eating well is the best revenge, and the recipes collected herein have been chosen with that in mind. These are our favourite recipes and those of our families and friends.

Our guidelines were that the dishes be simple, imaginative, and digestible. Don't expect to find exotic game birds floating in a cream and brandy sauce or lobster stuffed with caviar and foie gras.

These are the kind of wholesome, tasty dishes that would bring joy to the hearts of Butch Cassidy and Ernest Hemingway if the two of them happened to have dinner together.

—PAUL NEWMAN AND A. E. HOTCHNER

Starters

Paul Newman's Tomato and Endive Salad ▪ Tomato, Onion and Goat's Cheese Salad ▪ Paul's Caesar Salad ▪ Avocado and Feta Cheese with Lemon-Cumin Dressing ▪ Scallop and Prawn Salad with Shanghai Citrus Dressing ▪ Newman's Vinaigrette Dressing ▪ Fat-Free Sweet-Tart Mustard Dressing ▪ Cheese Puffs with Salsa Cream Filling ▪ Holly Hunter's Courgette Pancakes with Smoked Salmon and Yogurt-Dill Sauce ▪ Grilled Scallops with Avocado Cream and Salsa

I have two favorite appetizers. One is a dozen littleneck clams on the half-shell, topped with a squirt of lemon juice. The other one I've forgotten, but it probably has something to do with celery and/or beer.

I like any kind of melon as a starter, even watermelon, although melon is better eaten in the sauna or the shower, which makes me wonder whether it's an appetizer or a washcloth.

—Paul Newman

Newman as King Beer, Whoopi Goldberg as his queen, performing in the 1996 gala at the Hole in the Wall Gang Camp

Some people have sexual dreams, but I dream about salad. Then when I wake up, I want to eat the salad I dreamed about. (This morning I didn't eat anything because I dreamed about liver last night, and I hate liver.)

My salad dressing is literally something I dreamed up, the main part of it during a long night's sleep; the adjustments came in short afternoon naps.

—PAUL NEWMAN

Paul Newman's Tomato and Endive Salad

I like salads for lunch, and this one is at the top of my list. Of course, I use Newman's Own dressing on them, but if you have the questionable taste of preferring some others, suit yourself. ▪ **SERVES 4**

2 large, ripe fresh tomatoes	Newman's Own salad dressing or
250g (8oz) endive (about 3 medium)	Vinaigrette Dressing (page 30)
3 slices bacon	

Cut the tomatoes into small dice. Slice the endive to make 4 equal portions and mix with the tomatoes. Cook the bacon until very crisp. Crumble and then sprinkle over the salad. Toss with salad dressing to taste.

Tomato, Onion and Goat's Cheese Salad

If butterhead lettuce is not available, use lollo rosso. Soft-leaved lettuce of any kind is the way to go. Avoid anything too crunchy.

SERVES 6 TO 8 AS A STARTER

3 heads butterhead lettuce, leaves separated and 6 large outer leaves reserved for use as cups

2 heads radicchio, cut into julienne strips

3 tomatoes, cored and cut into quarters

1 small onion, finely chopped

125g (4oz) goat's cheese, crumbled

90–125ml (3–4fl oz) Newman's Own Balsamic Vinaigrette, or your favourite

In a large salad bowl, combine the lettuce, tomatoes, onion and goat's cheese. Add the dressing and toss well.

To serve, place a lettuce cup on each salad plate, then arrange the salad in and around it. Divide the tomatoes and goat's cheese evenly between the plates.

Paul's Caesar Salad
There's no raw egg in the dressing here! Classic or not, this is a mighty fine Caesar salad. If you're in a hurry, use preprepared romaine or cos hearts; they usually come three to a packet. You'll need two packets. Do take the time to make your own croûtons, though. They make a certifiable difference, as do great tomatoes (even if they are a non-traditional ingredient). ■ SERVES 6

CROÛTONS
½ French baguette, sliced into
    6 rounds about 4cm (1½in) thick
125g (4oz) unsalted butter, melted
2 tablespoons chopped garlic

SALAD
2 heads romaine or cos lettuce, torn
    into bite-sized pieces, or 2 packets
    romaine or cos hearts

125–175ml (4–6fl oz) Newman's Own
    Caesar Dressing, or your favourite
2 large, ripe beefsteak tomatoes, cored
    and cut into 6 slices each
90–100g (3–3½oz) Parmesan cheese,
    freshly grated, shaved or thinly
    sliced

To make the croûtons, dip each piece of bread into the melted butter. In a medium frying pan, combine the remaining butter with the garlic and heat until foamy. Add the bread rounds in 1 layer and brown lightly on both sides in the garlic butter, about 1 minute per side. Remove and reserve.

Toss the lettuce pieces in a bowl with about half the dressing. Arrange the lettuce on plates and add 2 tomato slices and 1 croûton per serving. Sprinkle with cheese or lay the shavings or slices on top. Serve the remaining dressing in a bowl.

Avocado and Feta Cheese with Lemon-Cumin Dressing

Don't be put off by what looks like large amounts of both vinegar and lemon juice in this dressing. The dressing *is* tangy, but it's great with this salad in particular and almost any other green salad as well. You will have quite a bit left over. It keeps for several weeks, covered, in the refrigerator.

You'll have half an avocado left over. We suggest eating it right on the spot. If that seems very aggressive, there's always the option of rubbing it with lemon juice, wrapping it tightly in clingfilm and hiding it in the refrigerator.

MAKES ABOUT 350ML (12FL OZ) DRESSING ■ SERVES 6

LEMON-CUMIN DRESSING

- 125ml (4fl oz) sherry vinegar
- 4 tablespoons fresh lemon juice
- 1 teaspoon French wholegrain mustard
- ¼ teaspoon chopped garlic
- 2 teaspoons ground cumin
- ½ teaspoon salt
- 1 teaspoon freshly ground black pepper
- 175ml (6fl oz) extra virgin olive oil

SALAD

- 4 small heads romaine or cos lettuce, outer leaves removed and discarded, inner leaves cut into julienne strips
- 5 plum tomatoes, chopped
- ½ small red onion, chopped
- 250g (8oz) feta cheese, crumbled
- 2 avocados

To make the lemon-cumin dressing, place all the ingredients except the oil in a blender and blend on high until combined. With the machine on low, add the oil in a slow, steady stream and blend for about 15 seconds, until combined.

To make the salad, combine all the ingredients in a large bowl except the avocados. Toss with about 75ml (3fl oz) of the dressing, adding more to taste if desired. Divide the salad between 6 salad plates.

Peel, stone and quarter the avocados, then cut each quarter, leaving it attached at the top, into thin slices. Fan the avocado slices, spreading them carefully on one side of each plate. (If you prefer, you can chop the avocados and add an equal amount to each salad.) Pour some of the remaining dressing into a bowl to spoon over the avocado.

Scallop and Prawn Salad with Shanghai Citrus Dressing

You'll have Shanghai citrus dressing left over after you make this salad. It shouldn't be a problem, though, because it is terrific as a basting sauce for grilled fish or shellfish. It is also excellent on Chinese chicken salad or on something as simple as plain roasted or grilled vegetables.

SERVES 6

SHANGHAI CITRUS DRESSING

4 tablespoons soy sauce

4 tablespoons fresh orange juice

6 tablespoons seasoned rice wine
    vinegar

2 tablespoons Dijon mustard

1 tablespoon honey

125ml (4fl oz) olive oil

¼ teaspoon salt

1 teaspoon freshly ground black
    pepper

1 tablespoon finely chopped coriander

SEAFOOD

12 scallops

6 large raw prawns, peeled and
    deveined

4 tablespoons olive oil

salt and freshly ground black pepper to
    taste

VEGETABLES

24 thin asparagus spears, ends
    trimmed and peeled

500g (1lb) mixed baby greens

1 cucumber, diced

½ small red onion, thinly sliced

To make the dressing, in a large bowl combine the soy sauce, orange juice, vinegar, mustard, and honey. Whisk together well. Add the oil in a slow, steady stream, whisking until fully incorporated. Whisk in the salt and pepper.

Prepare the seafood. Combine the scallops, prawns, 2 tablespoons of the oil, salt, and pepper in a bowl. Set aside at room temperature.

Prepare the vegetables. Bring a large pan of salted water to a rolling boil, add the asparagus spears, and blanch for 1 minute. Remove with a slotted spoon and place in a wide, shallow pan filled with iced water to stop the cooking and set the colour. Remove when cool and pat dry with kitchen paper. Chop the spears and combine with the baby greens, cucumber and onion in a large bowl.

To finish the seafood, heat 1 tablespoon of the remaining oil in a large frying pan or sauté pan over medium heat until hot. Add the scallops in 1 layer and cook for 5 minutes. Turn and cook 3 minutes more. Remove to a plate and set aside.

Pour the remaining tablespoon of oil into the pan, add the prawns and cook for a total of 5–7 minutes, turning, or until just cooked through.

Just before serving, stir the coriander into the dressing. Toss the salad with about 125ml (4fl oz) of the dressing, then divide among 6 plates. Top each serving with 2 scallops and 1 prawn. Season with salt and pepper. Serve with some of the remaining dressing to spoon over the shellfish.

Newman's Vinaigrette Dressing **Any oil and vinegar dressing (vinaigrette) can be used in the recipes in this book that call for Newman's Own.**

To make a basic vinaigrette, mix 1 part vinegar or lemon juice with 3 parts oil. Season with salt and pepper, and add Dijon mustard to taste. Use extra virgin olive oil and high-quality white or red wine vinegar for the best results. Vary the ratio of oil to vinegar for a sharper or milder dressing. You may add garlic (chopped or a whole peeled clove for subtle flavouring), dried or fresh herbs, or other seasonings. For variety try a herb vinegar in place of plain wine vinegar.

Fat-Free Sweet-Tart Mustard Dressing

The longer this dressing sits, the better it gets. Besides being fat-free, it is also multi-purpose. Use it as a dressing—on baby spinach leaves, for example—as a marinade for fish, poultry and meat, or as a dipping sauce. We've made a lot of it because you'll use a lot of it. It is not a recipe that should be made in smaller amounts; the flavour doesn't hold up when the amounts are reduced.

MAKES ABOUT 900ML (1 ½ PINTS)

200ml (7fl oz) French wholegrain mustard
200ml (7fl oz) Dijon mustard
200ml (7fl oz) honey mustard
4 tablespoons balsamic vinegar
1 tablespoon soy sauce
1 tablespoon fresh lemon juice

1 tablespoon fresh orange juice
1 teaspoon pure maple syrup
½ teaspoon salt
1 teaspoon freshly ground black pepper

Combine all the ingredients in a large jar or container with a lid. Stir together well until completely combined. Cover the jar and store it in the refrigerator. For best results, let the dressing stand 1 day in the refrigerator before using. Stir or shake before using.

The dressing will keep, covered and chilled, for 1 month.

Cheese Puffs with Salsa Cream Filling These

puffs are made with choux pastry, the same dough that is used for the great French dessert, eclairs. Unlike some French doughs, it is not hard to prepare, and is you want to make this really easy for yourself, bake the puffs in advance and freeze them. Defrost at room temperature and fill just before serving.

■ MAKES 36 PUFFS

DOUGH

75g (3oz) unsalted butter, cut into
    pieces
1 teaspoon salt
freshly ground black pepper to taste
freshly grated nutmeg to taste
    (optional)
125g (4oz) plain flour
4 large eggs plus 1 egg, lightly beaten,
    for the egg wash

125g (4oz) plus 3 tablespoons finely
    grated Cheddar or Swiss cheese

FILLING

one 325g (11oz) jar Newman's Own
    All-Natural Bandito Salsa, or your
    favourite
250g (8oz) cream cheese, whipped

Preheat the oven to 220°C, 425°F, gas mark 7. Grease 2 baking sheets.

To make the dough, place 250ml (8fl oz) of water in a large, heavy saucepan with the butter, salt, pepper and nutmeg. When the butter has melted and the water is boiling, re-move the pan from the heat and beat in the flour all at once with a wooden spoon. Stir vigorously until the mixture forms a ball and leaves the sides of the pan. (If it does not, return the pan to medium heat and beat vigorously for 1–2 minutes, until it forms a ball.) Off of the heat, beat in the 4 eggs, 1 at a time, until each is thoroughly incorpo-rated. Beat in the 125g (4oz) of grated cheese.

Transfer the dough to a piping bag fitted with a plain 1cm (½in) tip. Pipe rounds on the prepared baking sheets, each about 2.5cm (1in) in diameter, 2.5cm (1in) high, and 5cm (2in) apart. With a pastry brush, very carefully brush the tops of the rounds with some of the egg wash, taking care not to let any drip onto the baking sheets. (It will act like glue and prevent the puffs from puffing.) Sprinkle the remaining cheese over the tops of the rounds.

Bake for 20–25 minutes, or until golden and crisp. Remove from the oven and turn off the heat. With the tip of a small, sharp knife, pierce the top of each puff, then return the baking sheets to the oven to dry for 10 minutes. Remove and leave to cool on wire racks.

While the puffs are baking or as they cool, make the filling. Drain the salsa. In a bowl, combine the cream cheese with half of the drained salsa. Depending on how much of a salsa flavour you like, continue to add salsa to taste, blending it in well.

With a small, sharp knife, cut off the top half of the puffs. Spoon filling into each puff and place the tops of the puffs at a rakish angle.

Holly Hunter's Courgette Pancakes with Smoked Salmon and Yogurt-Dill Sauce

These are elegant and beautiful and make a great first or second course for brunch. You can also quarter the finished pancakes and serve them as an appetizer. Don't stint on the quality of smoked salmon. This is a case where more is more.

SERVES 6

YOGURT-DILL SAUCE

250ml (8fl oz) plain low-fat yogurt
4 tablespoons finely chopped fresh dill
salt and freshly ground black pepper
  to taste
juice of 1 lemon

PANCAKES

2 courgettes, ends trimmed
2 large baking potatoes, scrubbed but
  not peeled
1 small red onion, thinly sliced and cut
  into julienne strips
2 tablespoons olive oil

salt and freshly ground black pepper to
  taste
2 tablespoons vegetable oil for cooking
1½ teaspoons unsalted butter, melted,
  for cooking

ACCOMPANIMENTS

250g (8oz) mixed baby greens
375g (12oz) sliced smoked salmon (2
  slices per serving)
chopped chives for garnish
very thin lemon slices for garnish
freshly ground black pepper to taste

To make the sauce, combine all the ingredients in a ceramic or plastic bowl, cover and chill. (If you are making the sauce in advance, add the lemon juice just before serving, or the yogurt will separate.)

To make the pancakes, grate the courgettes and potatoes coarsely. Put the grated vegetables in a bowl and add the onion, olive oil, salt and pepper.

Preheat the oven to 150°C, 300°F, gas mark 2. Place 1 teaspoon of vegetable oil and ¼ teaspoon of melted butter in a 19cm (7½in) nonstick omelette pan over medium-high heat until hot. Add 75g (3oz) of the grated vegetables and spread the mixture to the edges of the pan, pressing down firmly with a rubber spatula to form a pancake about 5mm (¼ in) thick. Cook for about 3 minutes, until the edges begin to brown. Gently lift the pancake with the spatula, to check the underside. If it is deep golden brown in colour, turn (or flip) the pancake and cook for 3–4 minutes more, until golden. Transfer the pancake to a plate lined with kitchen paper to drain, then transfer to a baking sheet. Place in the oven to keep warm.

Make the remaining pancakes with ingredients in the same way, being sure to add 1 teaspoon of oil and a bit of butter to the pan before making each new pancake.

To serve, arrange some baby greens on 6 salad plates. Spread each pancake with about 2 tablespoons (or more to taste) of yogurt-dill sauce, then put a pancake on each plate on the greens. Arrange 2 slices of salmon on top of each pancake. Garnish each serving with some chives, several lemon slices, and a generous grinding of pepper. Serve the remaining sauce in a bowl.

Grilled Scallops with Avocado Cream and Salsa

As anyone who loves seviche knows, fresh lime and seafood were made for each other. Add a few other south-of-the-border ingredients like avocado, cumin and tortillas, and you have a dynamite dish.

■ MAKES 32 NIBBLES

4 tablespoons olive oil
3 tablespoons fresh lime juice
1½ teaspoons grated lime zest
¾– 1 teaspoon salt
½ teaspoon ground cumin
¼ teaspoon freshly ground black
   pepper
32 scallops

four 20cm ((8in) flour tortillas, cut into
   eighths (32 wedges)
2 firm, ripe avocados
1 small red onion, finely chopped
4 tablespoons plain low-fat or no-fat
   yogurt
250g (8oz) iceberg lettuce, shredded
175ml (6fl oz) Newman's Own All-
   Natural Bandito Salsa, or your
   favourite

In a medium ceramic or glass bowl, whisk together 2 tablespoons of oil, 2 tablespoons of lime juice, ½ teaspoon of grated zest, ¼ teaspoon of salt, the cumin and the pepper. Add the scallops and marinate, covered, in the refrigerator for 1 hour.

In a large nonstick frying pan, heat the remaining 2 tablespoons of oil over medium-high heat until hot. Add the tortilla wedges in batches and cook until golden brown on both sides, 1–2 minutes. Drain the wedges on kitchen paper.

Peel, stone and coarsely mash the avocados in another bowl. Stir in the onion, yogurt, and the remaining lime juice, zest and salt.

When ready to serve, preheat the grill. Cook the scallops in the grill pan about 7cm (3in) from the heat until cooked through, about 4–5 minutes.

To serve, spread 2 teaspoons of avocado cream on each tortilla wedge. Top with 1 table-spoon of lettuce and 1 scallop, and finish with about 1 teaspoon of salsa. Repeat with the remaining ingredients.

Soups, Stews and Chillies

Matthew Broderick's Tortilla Soup ▪ Nell Newman's Chicken Soup ▪ Nathan Lane's South-of-the-Border Courgette Soup ▪ Carole King's Sweet Pea Soup with Spicy Cream ▪ Roasted Squash Soup with Port ▪ Nell Newman's Cauliflower and Parmesan Soup with Essence of Lemon ▪ Joanne Woodward's Gazpacho ▪ Melissa Newman's Minestrone ▪ Butter Bean and Red Onion Soup ▪ Judge Roy's Zesty White Bean Bisque ▪ Franklin County, Florida's Own Frankly Fantastic Seafood Gumbo ▪ Towering Inferno Creole Posole ▪ Beef Stew with Potatoes and Pesto ▪ Robert Redford's Lamb Chilli with Black Beans ▪ Vegetarian Black Bean Chilli

Matthew Broderick's Tortilla Soup

This bold soup with big flavours is not for the lily-livered or faint of heart. We will let you adjust the amount of cumin and cilantro to suit your taste. Cold beer makes a very fine antidote; a crisp salad is a good accompaniment.

■ MAKES ABOUT 2 LITRES (3½ PINTS) ■ SERVES 6

3 large, very ripe tomatoes
4 tablespoons vegetable oil
4 tablespoons olive oil
4 large garlic cloves
1 onion, chopped
1 small jalapeño chilli, seeded and cut into strips
one 750g (24oz) can chopped, peeled tomatoes
4 tablespoons chilli powder
4 tablespoons ground cumin, or to taste
1 tablespoon garlic powder

8 tablespoons chopped coriander (or less, according to taste)
2 bay leaves
1.5–2 litres (2½-3½ pints) chicken stock
4 corn tortillas
salt and freshly ground black pepper to taste

GARNISH

unsalted corn chips, broken up
1 avocado, diced
6 teaspoons sour cream (optional)

Blacken the tomatoes in the vegetable oil in a very hot cast-iron frying pan or under the grill about 10cm (4in) from the heat. Turn with tongs until charred all over. (You can also char them without the oil, speared on the end of a long fork over an open gas burner.) Allow them to cool, then core and halve them.

Heat the olive oil in a stockpot over high heat until hot. Add the garlic and onion, cover, and cook over low heat for 3 minutes to soften. Add the jalapeño, canned tomatoes, blackened tomatoes, chilli powder, cumin, garlic powder, coriander, bay leaves and 1.5 litres (2½ pints) of the chicken stock. Add enough water to cover the ingredients by about 12cm (5in) and bring to the boil. Lower the heat and simmer the soup for 30 minutes.

While the soup is cooking, blacken the tortillas over an open grill or in a very hot un-oiled cast-iron frying pan. Leave to cool, then break up the tortillas and add them to the soup. Cook for 15 minutes. Remove the bay leaves.

Purée the hot soup in batches in a blender or food processor, filling the container only half-full each time. Blend on low, being sure to hold the lid down firmly. Return the soup to the pan and thin if necessary with the remaining chicken stock. Season the soup with salt and pepper and heat through.

Serve in bowls, garnished with the corn chips, avocado and sour cream.

And he asked himself—Good Lord, what have we unleashed?

—PAUL NEWMAN ON SEEING THE FIRST PROFIT AND
LOSS STATEMENT OF NEWMAN'S OWN

Nell Newman's Chicken Soup

My father has an inexhaustible fondness for soups and often makes quick-stop chicken soup with a prepared mix that he combines with noodles and fresh vegetables. In fact, give my father a hearty soup, a can of beer and a bag of popcorn, and he is as close to heaven as he can get.

He does handstands over my chicken soup, but in all fairness I must acknowledge that my recipe was inspired by the chicken soup our English governess, Duffy, made for us when we were little. ▪ SERVES 8 TO 10

STOCK

- 2 tablespoons olive oil
- 2 large leeks, well washed and the white parts chopped
- 3 carrots, sliced into 5mm (¼in) pieces
- 2 stalks celery, coarsely chopped
- 2 onions, coarsely chopped
- 4–6 garlic cloves, mashed
- 250ml (8fl oz) dry white wine
- 8 tablespoons finely chopped parsley
- 2 tablespoons finely chopped fresh marjoram
- 2–2.5kg (4–5lb) plump roasting chicken, cut into quarters, plus 2 thighs

CHICKEN SOUP

- 2 stalks celery, coarsely chopped
- 1 large leek, well washed and white part chopped
- 3 carrots, cut into 5mm (¼in) pieces
- 2 onions, coarsely chopped
- 150g (5oz) fresh or frozen peas
- 150g (5oz) fresh or frozen sweetcorn
- 1 bay leaf
- 8 tablespoons finely chopped parsley
- 2 tablespoons finely chopped fresh marjoram
- salt and freshly ground black pepper to taste
- egg noodles

To make the stock, heat the olive oil in a stockpot until hot. Add the leeks, carrots, celery, onions and garlic, and cook, stirring, until lightly browned. Add the wine, parsley, marjoram and 4.8 litres (8 pints) of cold water, and bring the mixture to the boil. Add the chicken and simmer for 1 hour. Remove the chicken breasts and allow to cool; then refrigerate. Continue simmering the stock for 3–4 hours. Remove from the heat and leave to cool. Strain the stock into a large bowl, and refrigerate.

When ready to serve, skim off all the fat from the stock and bring to the boil. Add all the vegetables and the bay leaf. Skin, bone and dice the breasts. Add to the pot with the parsley and marjoram. (You may want to add additional water at this point to thin the soup.) Finally, season with salt and pepper.

Meanwhile, in a separate pan, cook a generous amount of egg noodles, then drain them.

To serve, place a portion of cooked noodles in each soup bowl and ladle soup over the top. Serve with a crusty baguette or your favourite grilled cheese sandwiches as accompaniments.

Nathan Lane's South-of-the-Border Courgette Soup

There is no cream in this soup, but it still manages to have a creamy, wonderful texture. Try it with garlic bread and goat's cheese salad for a light lunch or supper. ■ MAKES 1.6 LITRES (2½ PINTS) ■ SERVES 8

4 tablespoons olive oil

1 bunch spring onions, ends trimmed and chopped

½ red onion, chopped

3 garlic cloves

2 tablespoons ground cumin

3 large or 4 medium courgettes, .75–1kg (1½–2lb), ends trimmed and quartered

1 small potato, peeled and diced

1.5 litres (2½ pints) vegetable or chicken stock

salt and freshly ground black pepper to taste

125g (4oz) low-fat Monterey Jack or Cheddar cheese, grated, to garnish

Newman, Nathan Lane, and the Hole in the Wall Gang Camp kids

Heat the olive oil in a large saucepan over high heat until hot but not smoking. Add the spring onions, onion, garlic and cumin, and cook, stirring, for 3 minutes. Add the courgettes, potato and stock, and bring to the boil. Lower the heat to medium and simmer for 40 minutes.

Purée the hot soup in a blender in batches, filling the container only half-full each time. Blend on low and be sure to hold the lid down firmly. Pour the soup back into the saucepan, season with salt and pepper, and reheat.

To serve, ladle the soup into 6 bowls and garnish each serving with 2 rounded tablespoons of grated cheese.

Carole King's Sweet Pea Soup with Spicy Cream

If you can't find mascarpone, one of Italy's richest cow's milk cheeses, don't just abandon making the spicy cream garnish; use sour cream instead. The subtle flavour that mascarpone adds makes it worth looking for; some well-stocked gourmet stores and supermarkets carry it.

■ **MAKES 1.6 LITRES (2½ PINTS)** ■ **SERVES 6**

SPICY CREAM

125g (4oz) mascarpone
juice of ¼ lemon
¼ teaspoon crushed red pepper flakes
¼ teaspoon freshly ground black
    pepper
pinch of salt

SOUP

2 tablespoons vegetable oil
10 garlic cloves
½ red onion, chopped
1 small carrot, chopped
1 small red potato, peeled and chopped
two 300g (10oz) packets frozen baby
    peas, defrosted, or 1kg (2lb) fresh
    peas, shelled
1.5–2 litres (2½–3½pints) vegetable or
    chicken stock
salt and freshly ground black pepper to
    taste

To make the spicy cream, combine all the ingredients in a small bowl. Cover and refrigerate until ready to use. The cream keeps, covered and chilled, for 2 days.

To make the soup, heat the oil in a large saucepan or stockpot over high heat until hot. Add the garlic and onion, and cook, stirring, for 5 minutes, or until the garlic is golden. Add the carrot, potato and peas and cook, stirring, for 3 minutes. Pour in 1.5 litres (2½ pints) of the stock and bring the mixture to a slow, rolling boil. Turn the heat to low and simmer for 45 minutes.

Purée the soup in a blender in batches, filling the container only half-full each time. Blend on low and be sure to hold the lid down firmly. Pour the soup back into the pan and thin it to the desired consistency with the remaining stock. Season with salt and pepper, and heat through.

Divide the soup among heated bowls and top each serving with a big spoonful of the spicy cream. Serve hot.

Roasted Squash Soup with Port

You may be lucky enough to find banana squash in your market, otherwise, butternut works just fine. This is a good autumn soup, filling but not rich—basically a vegetable stock purée. The toasted pumpkin seed garnish adds a lovely contrast of texture and flavour to the silky soup. ▪ MAKES ABOUT 2 LITRES (3½ PINTS) ▪ SERVES 6

1 large butternut squash, 2–2.5kg (4–5lb), halved and seeded
4 tablespoons vegetable oil
1 baking potato, peeled and chopped
1 onion, chopped
6 garlic cloves
1.5–2 litres (2½–3½pints) chicken stock

4 tablespoons ruby port
½ teaspoon ground allspice
salt and freshly ground black pepper to taste
25g (1oz) unsalted butter
toasted pumpkin seeds for garnish (optional)

Preheat the oven to 230°C, 450°F, gas mark 8.

Brush the cut surfaces of the squash with 2 tablespoons of the oil and place on a baking sheet. Bake until tender, about 45 minutes. Leave to cool, then scrape out the flesh into a bowl.

Heat the remaining 2 tablespoons of oil in a stockpot over high heat until hot. Add the potato, onion and garlic and cook, stirring, for 5 minutes. Add 1.5 litres (2½ pints) of the stock and bring to the boil. Stir in the cooked squash, port and allspice and cook at a low simmer for 40 minutes.

Purée the hot soup in a blender in batches, filling the container only half-full each time. Blend on low speed and be sure to hold the lid down firmly. Pour the soup back into the pot over low heat. Add more stock if necessary to arrive at the desired consistency. Add salt and pepper. Swirl in the butter.

Serve in soup bowls and garnish with the pumpkin seeds.

Nell Newman's Cauliflower and Parmesan Soup with Essence of Lemon

This is a fantastically fresh, slightly lemony soup with fresh green peas (not canned!) for colour. It goes very well with my Sesame Loaves (page 180). This soup originated during one of my refrigerator-cleaning sprees, in which I throw all my leftovers into a pan, heat them, and see what happens. ■ **MAKES ABOUT 2 LITRES (3½ PINTS)**

■ **SERVES 8 TO 10**

1 large cauliflower, 1–1.2kg (2–2¼lb), cut into 2.5cm (1in) pieces

1 onion, chopped

1.5 litres (2½ pints) chicken or vegetable stock

175g (6oz) uncooked millet

40g (1½oz) Parmesan cheese, freshly grated

juice of ½ lemon

175g (6oz) fresh peas, about 500g (1lb) peas, unshelled

salt and freshly ground pepper

Place the cauliflower in a stockpot along with the onion and stock. Simmer over medium heat until tender, about 15–20 minutes.

While the cauliflower is cooking, wash the millet in a strainer. Put into another pan with 600ml (1 pint) of water and cook over medium heat until soft and fluffy. (This may require a bit more water.)

When the cauliflower is cooked, place small batches in a blender or food processor along with the stock. Blend each batch until smooth. Return to the pot set over a low heat. Add the cheese, lemon juice, millet, peas, salt and pepper. Mix well and warm for 5 minutes before serving.

Joanne Woodward's Gazpacho

Don't throw out that leftover salad! Try this refreshing soup instead. You can include lettuce, tomato, cucumber, spring onions, onion, peppers and/or radishes.

■ MAKES ABOUT 1.25 LITRES (2 PINTS) ■ SERVES 4 TO 6

50g (2oz) leftover tossed salad with vinaigrette dressing
475ml (16fl oz) Newman's Own Sock-It-To-'Em Sockarooni Spaghetti Sauce, or your favourite meatless sauce

250ml (8fl oz) beef bouillon
chopped cucumber, spring onion and tomato for garnish (optional)

Puree the salad ingredients, sauce, and bouillon together in a blender or food processor. Add more bouillon if necessary to reach the desired consistency. Refrigerate for 1 hour.

Garnish each serving with the chopped cucumber, spring onion and tomato.

Melissa Newman's Minestrone
This hearty soup makes a meal with some crusty bread and a green salad. You can also sprinkle graated cheese on top. ■ MAKES 1.5 LITRES (2½ PINTS) ■ SERVES 8

125g (4oz) dried butter beans or kidney beans, soaked overnight, cooked until tender, and drained
1 large onion, chopped
1 stalk celery, chopped
1 carrot, chopped
¼ head green cabbage, shredded

125g (4oz) fresh peas
1 or 2 chicken or vegetable stock cubes
475ml (16fl oz) Newman's Own Sock-It-To-'Em Sockarooni Spaghetti Sauce, or your favourite meatless sauce

Simmer the beans, onion, celery, carrot, cabbage and peas in 750ml (1¼ pints) of water (or more if needed) with the stock cubes until the vegetables are tender, about 12–15 minutes. Add the sauce and simmer gently 5 minutes more. Serve hot.

Lissie, Paul Newman and Tony Randall at a Hole in the Wall Gang Camp gala

Butter Bean and Red Onion Soup

If you swore off butter beans a long time ago, try this substantial, flavourful soup and see if it isn't time for some revisionist thinking. Try it with Paul's Caesar Salad (page 26) for a light lunch or supper. This dish uses no dairy products, and there's not too much fat, either, which makes it politically correct, too.

■ MAKES ABOUT 1.25 LITRES (2 PINTS) ■ SERVES 6

4 tablespoons vegetable oil
1½ red onions, chopped
4 garlic cloves
two 300g (10oz) packs frozen baby
    butter beans, defrosted

1.25 litres (2 pints) chicken stock
salt and freshly ground black pepper to
    taste
chopped chives for garnish

Heat the oil in a large saucepan over high heat until hot. Add the onions and garlic, and cook, stirring, for 5 minutes. Add the beans and stock, and cook, stirring occasionally, for 30 minutes.

Purée the hot soup in a blender in batches, filling the container only half-full each time. Blend on low speed and be sure to hold the lid down firmly. Pour the soup back into the saucepan, season with salt and pepper, and reheat.

To serve, ladle the soup into each bowl and garnish with chives.

Judge Roy's Zesty White Bean Bisque

Paul says, 'Here's a recipe that will knock your socks off.' Tresa Rabchuk of Locust Valley, New York, adds a new twist to a classic creamy bean soup with the addition of Newman's Own Sock-It-To-'Em Sockarooni Spaghetti Sauce. The 1996 runner-up in the Newman's Own/*Good Housekeeping* Recipe Contest, her award went to the Animal Medical Center. ▪ MAKES 8 FIRST-COURSE SERVINGS

1 large onion, chopped

25g (1oz) unsalted butter or margarine

2 garlic cloves, crushed

250g (8oz) ham, diced

two 475–575g (15–19oz) cans white kidney beans, rinsed and drained

two 325g (11oz) cans sweetcorn, drained

475ml (16fl oz) single cream

250ml (8fl oz) Newman's Own Sock-It-to-'Em Sockarooni Spaghetti Sauce, or your favourite

250ml (8fl oz) water

1 teaspoon sugar

1 teaspoon dried thyme

1 teaspoon dried basil

½ teaspoon salt

½ teaspoon coarsely ground black pepper

½ teaspoon dried oregano

¼ teaspoon crushed red pepper flakes

1 bay leaf

In a large heavy pan sauté the onion in the butter over medium heat until tender and golden. Add the garlic and ham, and cook for 3 minutes. Add the remaining ingredients. Raise the heat to medium-high and bring to a boil, stirring. Remove the bay leaf before serving.

Franklin County, Florida's Own Frankly Fantastic Seafood Gumbo

Jackie Gay of Carrabelle, Florida, was the 1997 grand prize winner. She put on her lab coat for many an hour trying to achieve the perfect gumbo. Kudos to her for having created such a delectable combination of seafood and spices that any Cajun (or Yankee) would salute. She suggests serving crackers on the side and says that other seafoods can be substituted. Her award went to the Friends of the Franklin County Public Library. Warning: This makes enough to serve thirty-two people!

SERVES 32

2 tablespoons vegetable oil

4 large onions, sliced

4 red, green and yellow peppers, seeded and sliced

two 800g (26oz) jars Newman's Own All-Natural Diavolo Sauce, or your favourite spicy sauce

1 tablespoon Cajun seasoning

1 teaspoon freshly ground black pepper

1 teaspoon cayenne pepper

1½ teaspoons salt

600ml (1 pint) freshly shucked oysters with their juices

1kg (2lb) raw prawns, peeled and deveined

500g (1lb) scallops

500g (1lb) freshly cooked crab fingers, if available, or crabmeat

1kg (2lb) firm fish fillets, such as young cod, cut into 2.5cm (1in) pieces

500g (1lb) fresh or frozen sliced okra

2kg (4lb) hot, cooked, high-quality white rice

Heat the oil in a large, heavy saucepan over medium heat. Add the onions and peppers and cook until slightly soft. Drain off the excess oil. Add the sauce, 750ml (1¼ pints) water and all the seasonings. Turn the heat to low and simmer for 30 minutes. Add all the seafood and simmer for 45 minutes. Add the okra and simmer for 15 minutes. Serve immediately or refrigerate overnight.

To serve, reheat slowly, then put 60g (2⅓oz) of hot rice in each bowl and spoon the gumbo over it.

Towering Inferno Creole Posole

Alexandria Sanchez, who lives in Albuquerque, New Mexico, grew up on her Grandmother Sanchez's delicious posole. Now Alexandria has combined this traditional Mexican dish with the spicy flavours of Louisiana for a perfect blend of both cultures' cuisines. Along those lines, Alexandria suggests substituting 2 tablespoons 'Cajun Spice' for the last four ingredients in the seasoning mix.

This was the 1997 grand prize recipe, and Alexandria donated her award to Tree New Mexico, Inc. ■ SERVES 10

40g (1½oz) margarine or unsalted butter

250g (8oz) kielbasa (Polish sausage), cut into 1cm (½in) pieces

375g (12oz) boneless, skinless chicken breast, cut into bite-sized chunks

1 tablespoon chopped garlic

475ml (16fl oz) Newman's Own Sock-It-To-'Em Sockarooni Spaghetti Sauce, or your favourite

one to two 425g (14oz) cans chicken broth

one 900g (29oz) can white hominy, drained (look for Mexican-style or *para posole*)

one 475g (15oz) can black beans, drained and rinsed

sour cream for garnish

grated Monterey Jack or Cheddar cheese for garnish

SEASONING MIX

2 bay leaves

1½ teaspoons salt

1 teaspoon dried thyme

2 teaspoons red chilli powder or cayenne pepper

1 teaspoon white pepper

1 teaspoon freshly ground black pepper

1 teaspoon crushed red pepper flakes

VEGETABLE MIX

2 large stalks celery, chopped

1 onion, chopped

1 green pepper, seeded and chopped

Combine the ingredients for the seasoning mix.

Combine the ingredients for the vegetable mix.

Melt the margarine in a large, heavy saucepan over medium heat. Add the kielbasa and sauté until the pieces begin to brown, about 3 minutes. Add the chicken and sauté for 5 minutes. Add the seasoning mix, vegetable mix, and garlic, and sauté until the vegetables start to soften, about 10 minutes. Add the sauce, 250ml (8fl oz) of the chicken broth, the hominy and black beans. Cover and simmer over low heat, stirring occasionally, for 20 minutes. Add more chicken broth if the mixture seems too thick.

To serve, remove the bay leaves. Spoon the posole into large bowls, top with a dollop of sour cream, and sprinkle with the cheese. Serve with warm thick flour tortillas (not the type for rolling) or rice.

Beef Stew with Potatoes and Pesto

This is a really fresh-tasting, fragrant stew, redolent not only of pesto but lots of fresh parsley. If rump steak is not available, use another good-quality cut, such as boneless sirloin. Standard stew meat just does not cut it here. As everyone knows (and if they don't, they should), mashed potatoes are the only possible accompaniment, along with a bottle of bold red vino. ■ MAKES 250ML (8FL OZ) OF PESTO SAUCE ■ SERVES 6

4 small tomatoes
5 garlic cloves
2 tablespoons olive oil
1.15 litres (1¾ pints) beef stock
4 tablespoons vegetable oil
1 large red onion, diced
750g (1½lb) rump steak, cut into 2.5cm (1in) cubes
2 baking potatoes, peeled and cut into 1cm (½in) dice
125g (4oz) fresh or frozen sweetcorn
1 tablespoon Hungarian paprika
1 teaspoon ground coriander
1 bay leaf

salt and freshly ground black pepper to taste
8 tablespoons chopped parsley

PESTO SAUCE
50g (2oz) chopped basil leaves
3 garlic cloves, coarsely chopped
4 tablespoons fresh orange juice
4 tablespoons olive oil
25g (1oz) Parmesan cheese, freshly grated
1 tablespoon pine nuts
salt and freshly ground black pepper to taste

To make the pesto, combine half of all the ingredients, not including the salt and pepper, in a blender and blend until smooth. Set aside in a bowl. Repeat with the remaining ingredients. Combine the 2 batches and season with salt and pepper.

Preheat the grill.

Coat the tomatoes and garlic with olive oil and place on a baking sheet. Grill 10cm (4in) from the heat, turning with tongs, until blackened all over, about 10 minutes. Transfer the vegetables with the tongs to a blender. Add enough stock to blend until smooth.

Heat the vegetable oil in a pan over medium-high heat until hot. Add the onion and cook briefly, until soft. Add the beef and cook for 3 minutes, turning to brown evenly.

Add the potatoes, corn, paprika, coriander and bay leaf. Cook 3 minutes more, stirring to combine. Add the tomato-garlic purée and the remaining stock, bring to a boil, then turn the heat to low. Cook, stirring occasionally to prevent scorching, for 50 minutes, or until the potatoes are tender but not falling apart. Season well with salt and pepper. Stir in the parsley and cook for 2 minutes. Turn off the heat, remove the bay leaf, and stir in 6 tablespoons of the pesto.

Serve the stew in bowls garnished with a spoonful of the remaining pesto if desired.

Robert Redford's Lamb Chilli with Black Beans

You can substitute beef or even chicken in this chilli. Lamb does make it unusual and very good. It's the smoky flavour of the blackened tomatoes, though, that sends it over the top. ■ SERVES 6

3 large tomatoes
125ml (4fl oz) vegetable oil
6 garlic cloves
½ red onion, diced
750g (1½lb) lamb stew meat, cut into
    2.5–4cm (1–1½in) cubes
2 tablespoons chilli powder
1 tablespoon ground coriander
1 litre (1¾ pints) chicken stock
one 500g (16oz) can crushed tomatoes
1 tablespoon ketchup
1 tablespoon tomato paste

1 tablespoon Worcestershire sauce
175g (6oz) canned black beans,
    drained
pinch of dried mint
salt and freshly ground black pepper to
    taste

GARNISH

3 tablespoons chopped onion
3 tablespoons chopped spring onion
3 tablespoons sour cream
50g (2oz) pine nuts, toasted

Blacken the tomatoes in 4 tablespoons of oil in a very hot cast-iron frying pan or under the grill about 10cm (4in) from the heat, turning them with tongs until charred all over. (You can also char them without the oil; spear on the end of a long fork and hold over an open gas burner.)

Heat the remaining oil in a large saucepan over high heat until hot. Add the garlic, onion, lamb, chilli powder and coriander and cook, stirring, for 5 minutes. Add the blackened tomatoes, stock, crushed tomatoes, ketchup, tomato paste and Worcestershire sauce. Turn the heat to medium and cook, stirring occasionally, for 35 minutes. Add the beans, mint, salt and pepper. Turn the heat to medium-low and cook, stirring often to prevent scorching, for 10 minutes.

Serve the chilli in large bowls garnished with ½ tablespoon each of onion, spring onion and sour cream per serving. Pass the nuts separately.

Vegetarian Black Bean Chilli

Like most chillies and stews, this one gets better if left to stand overnight. To make a meal of this, you don't need much more than a good green salad, although a plate of Cornmeal Squares with Salsa (page 177) is a tasty addition. ■ SERVES 6

4 tablespoons vegetable oil

1 red onion, chopped

8 garlic cloves

1 large carrot, diced

175g (6oz) sweetcorn

2 tablespoons ground cumin

1 tablespoon chilli powder

1 bay leaf

¼ teaspoon crushed red pepper flakes (optional)

one 500g (16oz) can black beans, not drained

3 medium-large tomatoes, puréed

1.5 litres (2½ pints) vegetable stock

2 drops liquid smoke (optional)

250ml (8fl oz) stout

salt and freshly ground black pepper to taste

GARNISH

1 small red onion, finely chopped

6 teaspoons sour cream

1 avocado, peeled, stoned and diced

Heat the oil in a large saucepan over high heat until hot. Add the onion, garlic, carrot, corn, cumin, chilli powder, bay leaf and pepper flakes. Cook, stirring occasionally, for 5 minutes. Add the black beans, tomato purée and vegetable stock, and bring to a boil. Turn the heat to medium-low and simmer for 15 minutes. Stir well, add the liquid smoke, and simmer 15 minutes more. Add the beer and cook another 20 minutes, stirring every now and then. Season well with salt and pepper.

Serve in bowls and garnish with a teaspoon each of the red onion and sour cream and some diced avocado.

Main Courses

Butch's BBQ Sauce ▪ Matthew Broderick's Grilled T-bone Steak with Sweet Onion Marmalade and Campfire Mustard Sauce ▪ Danny Aiello's New York Sirloin Steak and His Cherokee Indian Curry AAA Steak Sauce ▪ Sundance's Salsa Steak in a Sack ▪ Whoopi Goldberg's Big Bad Ass Beef Ribs ▪ The Newmanburger ▪ Hud's Molasses-Grilled Pork with Port Wine Sauce ▪ Caroline Murphy's Ham Hocks and Beans ▪ Harry Belafonte's Pork, Apple and Yam Salad with Honey Mustard Dressing ▪ Lamb Chops with Minty Marinade ▪ Lamb Shanks Inferno ▪ Brutus' Lamb Tagine Marrakech ▪ Tony Randall's Grilled Veal

Chop with Bourbon–Cracked Black Pepper Sauce

Chicken with Orange Salsa Butter   Grilled Chicken

Paillards with Grilled Ratatouille and Romaine Hearts

Lemon Mustard Chicken   Caroline's Southern-Fried

Chicken   Martha Stewart's Chicken Cataplana

Chicken Cassidy Kebabs and the Sundance Orzo Pilaf

Greek Chicken Oregano Afloat in the Diavolo Drowning

Pool   Ismail Merchant's Yogurt Chicken   Hotch

Potch   Hotch's Chicken Marinara   Braised Chicken

with 'Say Cheese' Pasta Sauce, Mushrooms and Walnuts

   Grilled Cumin Chicken Salad   Cassidy's Chicken

Curry   Kiss of the Mediterranean Poussins

Incredible Cobb Salad   Spice-Rubbed Roasted Turkey

Breast ▪ The Grilled Bird of Youth Meets Judge Roy

Bean Salad ▪ Joanne Woodward's Sole Cabernet ▪

Joanne's Hollandaise Sauce ▪ Dilled Fillets of Cod à la

Newman ▪ Italian Baked Cod ▪ Mediterranean Fish

Fillets ▪ Herbed Salmon Fillets in Foil ▪ Salmon

Supper Salad ▪ Hotchner's Spanish Swordfish ▪

Walter Bridge's Grilled Swordfish Steaks ▪ James

Naughton's Honey Mustard Peppered Tuna Steaks ▪

The Hustler's Grilled Tuna Steaks with Caponata Relish

▪ Caroline Murphy's Tuna Salad ▪ Diavolo Seafood

Loaves ▪ Garlic-Herb Marinated Halibut with Lemon

Sauce ▪ Sarah Jessica Parker's Grilled Prawns with

Vodka-Lime Sauce ▪ Tasty Thai Prawn and Sesame

Noodles ▪ Piquant Scallops with Tangerines ▪

Joanne Woodward's Cioppino ▪ Blaze's Prawn and

Sausage Creole ▪ Cool Hand Luke's Brunch Burrito ▪

The Woodward Veggyburger ▪ Twice-Baked Potato

over Spinach, Broccoli and Peppers ▪ Nell Newman's

Marinated Ginger Tofu over Crispy Browned Soba

Noodles ▪ Potato and Cheese Quesadillas with Green

and Red Sauces ▪ Piñata Pockets

Pit Stop Pot Roast
Submitted by Sally Blitsch, Waterloo, Iowa

■ **SERVES 5**

1.5kg (3lb) pot roast of beef	aluminum foil
250ml (8fl oz) Newman's Own Light Italian Salad Dressing	nonflammable cord
	200-mile trip

Twelve hours before the onset of the trip, place the roast in a glass bowl and cover the meat entirely with the dressing.

Place the roast on the aluminum foil. Wrap the roast in the foil and seal *tightly* on the top and at each end.

Fasten the wrapped meat securely on top of the manifold of the car or truck engine. Get into the car, fasten your seat belts, and begin your trip.

After 100 miles, turn the roast. Continue on the last 100 miles of the trip. At the end of the trip, the roast should be done and delicious.

If we ever have a plan, we're screwed!

—PAUL NEWMAN TO THE CHIEF
AUDITOR OF THE IRS

Butch's BBQ Sauce

Butch's BBQ Sauce There are many ingredients in this sauce, but once you make a batch of it, you'll have plenty on hand to use any time you like. It's a keeper in the refrigerator and freezes well, too. You might even consider splitting a batch and storing half in the refrigerator, half in the freezer.

This sauce figures prominently in a few four-star recipes in this chapter: Danny Aiello's New York Sirloin Steak and his Cherokee Indian Curry AAA Steak Sauce (page 65) and Whoopi Goldberg's Big Bad Ass Beef Ribs (page 68). A spoonful or two isn't bad on a well-constructed Newmanburger, either (page 69).

Don't confuse creamy horseradish sauce with the plain grated variety. You want a prepared creamy sauce here; it's usually sold in the condiment section of the supermarket. The garlic granules are also found in many supermarkets. ■ MAKES 1.75–2 LITRES (3–3 ½ PINTS)

125ml (4fl oz) rapeseed oil	125g (4oz) tomato paste
50g (2oz) onion, chopped	125ml (4fl oz) balsamic vinegar
16 garlic cloves, chopped	125ml (4fl oz) Dijon mustard
1 litre (1¾ pints) tomato purée	4 tablespoons dark molasses
175g (6oz) dark brown sugar	4 tablespoons dried onion
250ml (8fl oz) Worcestershire sauce	4 tablespoons garlic granules
250ml (8fl oz) clover honey	2 teaspoons salt
250ml (8fl oz) ketchup	1 tablespoon freshly ground black
125ml (4fl oz) creamy horseradish	pepper
sauce	1 bay leaf

Heat the oil in a large saucepan over medium-high heat until hot. Add the chopped onion and garlic, and cook, stirring, about 1 minute.

Add all the remaining ingredients and 600ml (1 pint) of water. Bring to the boil, stirring to dissolve the sugar. Simmer, stirring occasionally, for 20 minutes. Remove the bay leaf and leave to cool.

The sauce will keep in a covered container in the refrigerator for 2 months.

Matthew Broderick's Grilled T-bone Steak with Sweet Onion Marmalade and Campfire Mustard Sauce

Steak doesn't get any better than this, and when paired with Roasted Herbed New Potatoes with Spinach (page 166), it tastes too good to be true. If this seems like a lot of work, remember that both the marmalade and the campfire mustard sauce can be made up to four days in advance. Keep covered in the refrigerator. Then it's just a question of making the potatoes and grilling the steaks. It's well worth the effort.

SERVES 6

six 375–425g (12–14oz) T-bone steaks
salt and freshly ground black pepper to
   taste

ONION MARMALADE

25g (1oz) unsalted butter
4 onions, thinly sliced
6 shallots, thinly sliced
10 garlic cloves, thinly sliced
125ml (4fl oz) port
4 tablespoons balsamic vinegar

CAMPFIRE MUSTARD SAUCE

6 tablespoons Dijon mustard
6 tablespoons French wholegrain
   mustard
6 tablespoons honey mustard
4 tablespoons balsamic vinegar
1 teaspoon freshly ground black
   pepper

Bring the steaks to room temperature, then season with salt and pepper.

Meanwhile, make the onion marmalade. Melt the butter in a large cast-iron frying pan. Add the onions, shallots and garlic and cook over high heat, stirring, for 10 minutes, until the onions are soft. Add the port and vinegar, and cook about 5–10 minutes, until the liquid is almost evaporated. Remove the pan from the heat but keep the marmalade warm.

To make the mustard sauce, combine all the ingredients in a bowl.

Preheat the grill until hot. Grill the steaks for 4–4½ minutes per side for rare, 6–7 minutes per side for medium-rare.

Serve each steak topped with some warm marmalade. Serve the mustard sauce separately in a bowl.

Danny Aiello's New York Sirloin Steak and His Cherokee Indian Curry AAA Steak Sauce

It shouldn't take you more than about ten minutes to put this dynamite steak sauce together—which means you will have time to make Yam Gratin (page 170) and Caramelized East Indian Vegetables (page 162), both of which go stupendously well with these steaks. It also means you have a lot of really good eating in store.

You can find the red curry powder in specialist Indian shops.

Leftover steak sauce will keep, covered and refrigerated, for about two weeks. Try it on chicken, too. ▪ MAKES ABOUT 750ML (1¼ PINTS)
▪ SERVES 6

CHEROKEE INDIAN CURRY AAA STEAK SAUCE

250ml (8fl oz) Butch's BBQ Sauce (see page 63), or your favourite brand
125ml (4fl oz) red wine vinegar
125ml (4fl oz) orange juice concentrate
4 tablespoons fresh lime juice
4 tablespoons vegetable oil
2½ tablespoons Madras curry powder
1 teaspoon red curry powder
1 teaspoon ground coriander

½ teaspoon salt
1 teaspoon freshly ground black pepper
¼ teaspoon ground allspice
1 tablespoon chopped garlic

six 250–300g (8–10oz) sirloin steaks, 2.5cm (1in) thick)
salt and freshly ground black pepper to taste

To make the steak sauce, combine all the ingredients in a large saucepan and add 125ml (4fl oz) of water. Cook over medium heat for 15 minutes. Leave to cool.

Place the steaks in a large shallow dish in 1 layer. Add 475ml (16fl oz) of the steak sauce and marinate for 30 minutes at room temperature. Turn and marinate for 30 minutes longer.

Grill or pan-fry the steaks to the desired doneness. Season with salt and pepper, and serve.

Sundance's Salsa Steak in a Sack

Julie DeMatteo, a 1992 finalist, was inspired by Paul Newman's movie *Butch Cassidy and the Sundance Kid* to create a recipe worth its weight in gold—golden bundles of filo pastry with fillet steak and salsa inside. Julie donated her award to Catholic Charities of Trenton and the Respiratory Distress Syndrome Foundation.

■ **SERVES 4**

four 125g (4oz) fillet steaks, 2.5cm (1in) thick
½ teaspoon salt
½ teaspoon freshly ground black pepper
1 teaspoon olive oil
4 spring onions
melted butter, for brushing

12 sheets filo pastry, 42 x 30cm (17 x 12in)
4 whole mild green chillies (from a 125g (4oz) can)
one 325g (11oz) jar Newman's Own All-Natural Bandito Salsa, or your favourite

Make a horizontal slit in each steak. Sprinkle the cut surfaces with salt and pepper, and reclose the steaks. Pan-fry in the oil over medium-high heat for 1 minute on each side, or until well browned. Transfer to a plate.

Cut the white part off each spring onion and halve lengthwise. Cut the green part of 1 spring onion into 4 lengthwise strips.

Preheat the oven to 190°C, 375°F, gas mark 5. Lightly brush a baking sheet with melted butter.

Place 1 sheet of filo pastry on a clean, dry, flat surface. (Keep the remaining sheets from drying out by covering them with damp kitchen paper.) Lightly brush the sheet with melted butter, then fold in half lengthwise, buttered side down. Place 1 steak in the centre of the sheet. Insert 2 white pieces of spring onion, 1 chilli and 125ml (4fl oz) of salsa inside the steak. Fold the pastry over, forming a bundle, and brush all over with melted butter. Place another sheet of filo on the work surface and brush with melted butter. Top with a second sheet of filo and brush again. Place the steak bundle in the centre of the stacked sheets and gather them around the bundle, gently pressing it together in the centre so that the bundle resembles a sack tied in the middle. Tie a green strip of spring onion around the gathered part of the bundle.

Make 3 more bundles in the same way.

Place the 4 bundles on the prepared baking sheet and brush the bundles with melted butter again. Bake the bundles for 20 minutes, or until golden brown. (The meat will be well done.)

Serve with the remaining salsa.

You can get straight A's in marketing and still flunk ordinary life.

—PAUL NEWMAN TO LEE IACOCCA AFTER
IACOCCA'S PINTO CAUGHT FIRE

Whoopi Goldberg's Big Bad Ass Beef Ribs

Excellent with **Potato Salad with Two Mustards Dressing** (page 167). You'll have leftover marinade; use it in the same way you would any great steak marinade.

MAKES 900ML (1 ½ PINTS) OF MARINADE ▧ **SERVES 6**

18 beef ribs (not short ribs)

MARINADE

475ml (16fl oz) Butch's BBQ Sauce
(page 63), or your favourite brand
125ml (4fl oz) Worcestershire sauce
75ml (3fl oz) fresh lemon juice
4 tablespoons Dijon mustard

2 tablespoons orange juice concentrate
2 tablespoons chopped garlic
1 tablespoon dark brown sugar
1 teaspoon dried thyme
½ teaspoon salt
1 tablespoon freshly ground black
   pepper
1 teaspoon natural smoke flavouring

Place the ribs in a large saucepan of cold water and bring to the boil. Simmer, uncovered, for 45 minutes.

While the ribs are cooking, combine all the marinade ingredients in a large saucepan and bring to the boil. Simmer, stirring occasionally, for 15 minutes.

Preheat the oven to 160°C, 325°F, gas mark 3.

Drain the ribs and arrange in 1 layer in a large roasting tin. Pour 475ml (16fl oz) of marinade over them, brushing it on to cover both sides. Bake for 30–40 minutes, until the ribs are tender.

Serve with lots of napkins and a bowl of the remaining marinade on the side.

Newman and Whoopi at a camp gala

The Newmanburger

Don't make the mistake of using minced rump or sirloin in this recipe; many hamburger cooks fall short of my standards because they use meat that is simply too good. I cook all my hamburgers on the barbecue or indoor fireplace grill, and chuck steak is best suited to a hot charcoal fire.

chuck steak, minced	tomatoes, sliced
vegetable oil	onion, thinly sliced
hamburger buns	kosher dill pickles, slivered

Form the chuck into hamburger patties of the preferred size. I toss them from hand to hand to keep them fluffy. Never pat down the meat, or the hamburger won't be able to breathe while it's cooking. Also, never put salt, pepper or any other seasoning in the meat before cooking because that will toughen it. The idea of adding onions, eggs, breadcrumbs, or any other ingredient to the meat raises my hackles. Never confuse steak tartare with the pure hamburger.

Prepare the charcoal and grease the grill with vegetable oil, but don't put the meat on the fire until the charcoal is a uniform greyish white. Sear the burgers well on 1 side and turn them only once. After turning them, lower the grill for a brief time to sear the meat. The result: a hamburger that is crisp on the outside, tomato-red inside.

While the Newmanburgers are cooking, toast the buns around the edge of the grill. At my house, tomatoes, sliced onions and pickles are the inevitable accompaniments. If corn is in season, it is also made part of the meal, always cooked for precisely 3 minutes and not a second longer in boiling, sweetened water. And a huge salad bowl, brimming with whatever fresh makings the market has to offer, is the table's centrepiece.

Although the Newmanburger is usually accompanied by frosty mugs of beer, on occasional impulse I serve up a bottle of Mouton-Rothschild or its equivalent, and that's when the Newmanburger tastes its best!

Hud's Molasses-Grilled Pork with Port Wine Sauce

Marie Terran, a 1996 runner-up, likes experimenting with food and made several attempts before finding the right balance of flavours to enhance but not overwhelm pork tenderloin. This recipe is sure to please Hud or that special someone. Marie donated her award to Aging Services for the Upper Cumberlands, Inc. ■ SERVES 6

175ml (6fl oz) light molasses

175ml (6fl oz) Newman's Own Olive Oil and Vinegar Dressing, or your favourite

750–875g (1½–1¾lb) whole pork tenderloin

1 tablespoon cracked black peppercorns

1 tablespoon cornflour

2 tablespoons chicken stock

SAUCE

175ml (6fl oz) port

75g (3oz) dried cranberries, or tart cherries or raisins

2 tablespoons Newman's Own Olive Oil and Vinegar Dressing, or your favourite vinaigrette

1 tablespoon finely chopped shallot

350ml (12fl oz) chicken stock

⅛ teaspoon cayenne pepper

To prepare the pork, mix the molasses and dressing in a self-sealing plastic bag. Add the pork tenderloin and seal the bag, pressing out as much air as possible. Marinate the pork in the refrigerator for at least 1 hour, turning occasionally.

To make the sauce, in a small bowl mix together the port and cranberries. Set aside.

In a saucepan, heat the 2 tablespoons dressing over medium heat, add the shallot, and cook for 2–3 minutes.

Drain the cranberries in a sieve set over a cup, pressing down on them to remove the port. Add the port to the hot dressing and bring the mixture to the boil over high heat. Boil for 1 minute, until reduced to 4 tablespoons. Add the chicken stock, cranberries and cayenne pepper and bring to the boil. Lower the heat to a simmer and cook the sauce until reduced by about half, 15–20 minutes.

While the sauce is simmering, light the barbecue.

Remove the pork from the marinade, reserving the marinade. Roll the pork in the cracked peppercorns, then place on the hot grill of the barbecue and sear over high heat. Lower the heat to medium and cook, turning and basting with the marinade every 5 minutes, for about 12–15 minutes, until the pork just loses its pink colour. Remove and thinly slice.

Mix the cornflour into the 2 tablespoons of stock. Stir the mixture into the reduced port sauce and bring to the boil. Remove the pan from the heat and serve the sauce over the pork.

It is useless to put on your brakes when you are upside down.

—PAUL NEWMAN TO A. E. HOTCHNER
AT THE SCENE OF THE CRASH

Caroline Murphy's Ham Hocks and Beans

My three favourite dishes all happen to be the culinary creations of my own household, which is, of course, gastronomically incestuous. Here's the recipe for my housekeeper's ham hocks and butter beans, which I would kill for.

▓ **SERVES 4**

4 smoked ham hocks four 300g (10oz) packs frozen broad beans	freshly ground black pepper

Cook the ham hocks in enough water to cover until almost tender. This will take 1–2 hours. Add the butter beans and pepper to taste. Cook until the beans are tender.

The only problem with this dish is that the ham hocks must be of top quality with lots of meat on them, and good ham hocks are hard to find. But if you tell your butcher in advance, he can usually turn up some good ones for you.

Harry Belafonte's Pork, Apple and Yam Salad with Honey Mustard Dressing

Jalapeño Spoon Bread (page 175) was made for this salad. Time the two dishes so that you can serve the spoon bread warm—the only way to serve it. Start the spoon bread first, and while it is baking, put this warm salad together. It's easy to make and surprisingly light. Note that there is no oil in the dressing at all. If you can't get a Cox's pippin or other pippin, use Granny Smith's.

■ MAKES ABOUT 175ML (6FL OZ) OF DRESSING ■ SERVES 6

DRESSING

- 125g (4fl oz) honey mustard
- 2 tablespoons Worcestershire sauce
- 1 tablespoon balsamic vinegar
- 1 tablespoon freshly ground black pepper
- 1 teaspoon salt

SALAD

- 6 strips bacon, chopped, cooked and drained, with drippings reserved
- 1.15kg (2¼lb) pork tenderloin, diced
- 2 tablespoons olive oil
- 1 large yam, peeled and diced
- 1 Cox's pippin, unpeeled, cored and diced

To make the dressing, combine all the ingredients in a small bowl.

To make the salad, put the bacon in a large serving bowl. Heat the drippings in a frying pan until hot. Add the diced pork and cook, tossing, until barely medium-rare, about 3 minutes. Remove to a bowl.

Wipe the frying pan clean, add the oil, and heat until hot. Add the yam and sauté until almost soft, about 5 minutes. Add the apple and cook, tossing, for 1 minute. Add to the serving bowl with the bacon.

Return the pork to the skillet and finish cooking it, tossing, for about 7 minutes. Immediately add the pork to the serving bowl, pour in the dressing, and toss.

Serve at once while the pork is still warm.

Lamb Chops with Minty Marinade

Suggesting a cooking time for meat is a tricky issue. One person's medium is another's well done. With a cut as extravagant as double-thick lamb chops, err on the side of undercooking. You can always cook them a little more. The best way to judge when meat is properly cooked is by hand, something all good chefs do instinctively. When you think the meat you're cooking is done, press down on the thickest part with your finger. The meat will bounce back slowly for rare. The longer the meat cooks, the faster it will regain its shape. For well done there will be no indentation at all.

Make Garlicky Mashed Potatoes (page 164) to go with these chops.

▨ MAKES ABOUT 350ML (12FL OZ) OF MARINADE ▨ SERVES 6

12 double-thick rib lamb chops,
175–200g (6–7oz) each
salt and freshly ground black pepper
olive oil for searing the chops

MARINADE
175ml (6fl oz) mint Worcestershire
sauce
125ml (4fl oz) olive oil
4 tablespoons balsamic vinegar

4 tablespoons fresh orange juice
juice of 2 lemons
1 small onion, chopped
1 tablespoon finely chopped mint leaves
1 teaspoon chopped garlic
1 teaspoon ground cumin
1 teaspoon ground ginger
1 teaspoon salt
1 tablespoon freshly ground black
pepper

To make the marinade, mix all the ingredients together well in a large glass bowl or jar. The marinade will keep, covered and refrigerated, for 2 weeks.

Season the chops with salt and pepper, then arrange in a single layer in a large shallow dish. Pour in 250ml (8fl oz) of the marinade and leave for 1 hour at room temperature.

To grill or roast the chops, preheat the grill or oven to 200°C, 400°F, gas mark 6. If roasting, heat 2 tablespoons of the oil in each of 2 cast-iron frying pans until hot. Add the chops and sear on both sides until golden. Transfer the pans to the oven and roast for 5 minutes on each side for rare, 7–8 minutes on each side for medium-rare. If grilling, cook the chops for 9 minutes on each side or to the desired degree of doneness.

Serve 2 chops per person, with about 2 tablespoons of marinade spooned over the meat.

Lamb Shanks Inferno

Sue Bloom of Rhinebeck, New York, won the 1994 grand prize with this spicy dish. Sue donated her award to the Tufts University School of Veterinary Medicine.

Serve with mashed potatoes, egg noodles or rice. ■ SERVES 4

4 lamb shanks
salt and freshly ground black pepper to
    taste
25g (1oz) flour
6 tablespoons olive oil
1 small onion, diced
2 garlic cloves, finely chopped

1 carrot, diced
175ml (6fl oz) dry red wine
175ml (6fl oz) beef stock
one 800g (26oz) jar Newman's Own
    All-Natural Diavolo Sauce, or your
    favourite spicy sauce
parsley sprigs for garnish

Preheat the oven to 180°C, 350°F, gas mark 4.

Season the lamb shanks with salt and pepper and dredge them in the flour; tap off the excess. Heat 5 tablespoons of the oil in a large casserole dish until medium-hot. Add 2 of the lamb shanks, brown them all over, then set aside. Repeat with the remaining 2 lamb shanks.

Scrape the brown bits off the bottom of the casserole and discard. Heat the remaining 1 tablespoon of oil in the casserole until medium-hot. Add the onion and garlic and sauté until soft and translucent. Add the carrot and sauté for 1–2 minutes. Add the red wine, raise the heat to high, and reduce the wine by half. Add the beef stock and sauce and bring just to the boil. Immediately remove the casserole from the heat.

Add the lamb shanks to the casserole, spoon the sauce over them, and cover tightly. Bake for 2 hours, or until the meat is tender.

Remove the shanks and keep them warm. Skim the fat from the sauce. Adjust the seasonings.

Serve the lamb shanks with the sauce and garnish with the parsley sprigs.

Brutus' Lamb Tagine Marrakech

Newman's Own Caesar Dressing serves as the perfect marinade for shoulder of lamb. It is then presented in a flavourful sauce featuring prunes marinated in sherry, mixed with a mélange of spices, and Newman's Own All-Natural Bandito Salsa. 'Tagine' is the Moroccan word for stew, hence Marrakech.

Barbara Morgan, 1995 runner-up, donated her award to the Enchanted Hills Summer Camp for the Blind. ■ MAKES ABOUT 250ML (8FL OZ) OF SAUCE ■ SERVES 12

375g (12oz) stoned prunes
150ml (¼ pint) dry sherry
1.5kg (3lb) lean shoulder of lamb, cut into 4cm (1½in) cubes
one 250g (8oz) bottle Newman's Own Caesar Dressing, or your favourite
2 large onions, finely chopped
3 garlic cloves, finely chopped
1 small knob of root ginger, peeled and shredded
1–2 teaspoons finely chopped jalapeño chilli
two 425–475g (13¾–14½oz) cans chicken broth

3 carrots, peeled and sliced
2 baking potatoes, peeled and diced
125ml (4fl oz) Newman's Own All-Natural Bandito Salsa (Medium), or your favourite
2 tablespoons fresh lemon juice
1 tablespoon chopped fresh thyme
1 tablespoon ground cumin
1 teaspoon ground turmeric
1 teaspoon Hungarian paprika
2 tablespoons chopped coriander

Preheat the oven to 190°C, 375°F, gas mark 5. Cover the prunes with the sherry and soak for 15 minutes or longer.

Place the lamb cubes and dressing in an airtight container or plastic bag and coat the cubes thoroughly. Marinate in the closed container for at least 1 hour in the refrigerator.

Remove the lamb from the marinade with a slotted spoon and discard the marinade. In a 30cm (12in) frying pan, brown the lamb in batches over medium-high heat, then transfer to a large casserole.

Using the same frying pan, sauté the onions over medium heat for 10 minutes. Add the garlic and sauté for 3 minutes more. When the onions are translucent, mix in the ginger root and jalapeño and cook for 2 minutes. Transfer the mixture to the casserole.

Add the broth, carrots, potatoes, salsa, lemon juice, thyme, cumin, turmeric and paprika and bring to the boil. Add the prunes with the sherry. Cover and bake for 45 minutes, or until the lamb and vegetables are tender. Stir in the coriander.

Serve over egg noodles.

Just when things look darkest they go black.

—PAUL NEWMAN TO
WALTER MONDALE, 1984

Tony Randall's Grilled Veal Chop with Bourbon-Cracked Black Pepper Sauce

A peppery bourbon butter sauce enhances the subtle flavour of veal here. Serve with Braised Root Vegetables (page 169); they look good on the plate, taste great, and come in handy when you're hunting down the last of this blue-ribbon sauce. ■ SERVES 6

6 veal chops, 300–375g (10–12oz) each
salt and freshly ground black pepper to
    taste
2 tablespoons olive oil

BOURBON SAUCE

4 tablespoons dry red wine
4 tablespoons dry white wine

125ml (4fl oz) bourbon
125g (4oz) cold unsalted butter, cut into
    large dice
salt to taste
1½ teaspoons coarsely cracked fresh
    black pepper

Light the barbecue and leave until hot or preheat the oven to 180°C, 350°F, gas mark 4.

Season the veal chops well with salt and pepper.

If you are grilling the chops, rub them with the oil. Place on the barbecue grill, leaving space between. Grill for 7–10 minutes on each side, turning once. If the chops are 4cm (1½in) thick, cook for 9–12 minutes on each side.

If you are roasting the chops, heat the oil in a large cast-iron frying pan over high heat until hot. Add the chops and sear on 1 side only. Transfer the pan to the oven and roast the chops for 10–12 minutes more for medium-rare.

While the chops are cooking, make the sauce. Combine the red and white wines in an enamel saucepan and cook over high heat until hot. Add the bourbon and cook until reduced by half.

Lower the heat to medium and add the butter, 1 piece at a time, quickly whisking it in until completely incorporated. Blend in each piece of butter fully, not just melt it, before adding the next. Work quickly but do not increase the heat under the sauce. Season with salt and cracked black pepper, and keep warm in a bain-marie until ready to use. Do not reheat the sauce over direct heat.

Place a grilled chop on each dinner plate and spoon about 2 tablespoons of the bourbon sauce over the top. Serve immediately.

Tony in the camp's skewed version of Cinderella

Chicken with Orange Salsa Butter
Salsa and a little orange zest perk up the mild flavour of white meat chicken. This is quick and good, and as mild or spicy as the salsa you use. Serve over pilaf or spinach pasta. ■ SERVES 4

4 tablespoons unsalted butter at room temperature

4 tablespoons Newman's Own All-Natural Bandito Salsa, or your favourite

1 teaspoon grated orange zest

50g (2oz) flour

½ teaspoon salt

¼ teaspoon cayenne pepper

2 chicken breasts, 250g (8oz) each, skinned, boned and halved

4 tablespoons fresh orange juice

2 tablespoons vegetable oil

orange slices for garnish

In a food processor, process the butter, salsa and orange zest until smooth. Spoon the butter onto a sheet of clingfilm and shape into a log. Wrap tightly and freeze.

Combine the flour, salt and cayenne on a plate.

Dip the chicken pieces, 1 at a time, in the orange juice and then in the seasoned flour; shake off the excess. Discard the juice.

Heat the oil in a large nonstick frying pan over medium-high heat. Add the chicken in 1 layer and cook, turning once, until golden brown and cooked through, about 7–8 minutes depending on thickness. Place on dinner plates.

Cut the cold orange butter into 4 pieces and put a piece on each chicken breast. Garnish with orange slices and serve at once.

Dear Sirs:

A miracle happened while eating a salad with your delicious dressing. Some dropped on my shoe. I ran and got kitchen paper and rubbed it off—haven't seen a shine on my shoes like that for 81 years. Now I use it every day for shining my shoes and putting on my salad. Even tried it on furniture, and it worked. So you have a product to double your money. Your sales would go up 10 per cent if you let people know your dressing is good for shoes and furniture polish.

With your knowledge of products, I am sure you could make a cake out of it for shoe shining.

J.F.

Grilled Chicken Paillards with Grilled Ratatouille and Romaine Hearts

Arnauld Briand, former executive chef of the Rainbow Room complex atop Rockefeller Center in New York City, created this elegant yet lean dish. ▪ SERVES 4

4 skinless, boneless chicken breasts
freshly ground black pepper
one and a half 250g (8oz) bottles Newman's Own Light Italian Dressing, or your favourite dressing
2 tablespoons finely chopped garlic
2 sweet onions, cut into thick slices

1 courgette, cut into 5mm (¼in) slices
1 yellow squash, cut into 5mm (¼in) slices
1 medium aubergine, cut into 1cm (½in) slices
2 heads Romaine or cos lettuce
cherry tomatoes
fresh herbs

Pound the chicken breasts into escalopes, about 5mm (¼in) thick. Sprinkle with pepper and marinate in 125ml (4fl oz) of dressing and 1 tablespoon of garlic for 2 hours.

Marinate the onions, courgette, squash and aubergine in 125ml (4fl oz) of the dressing and the remaining 1 tablespoon of garlic.

Light the barbecue.

Grill the chicken breasts and vegetables over hot coals until charred but not burned and the chicken is cooked through, about 3 minutes on each side.

Arrange the grilled vegetables on 4 plates, leaving the centre empty. Remove the outside leaves of the lettuce and chop the hearts. Place the chopped lettuce in the centre of each plate. Place the grilled chicken on the lettuce and spoon some of the remaining dressing over the top. Garnish with the cherry tomatoes and fresh herbs.

Lemon Mustard Chicken

Mustard and chicken go together, and lemon and chicken do too, so it follows that mustard, lemon and chicken would make an excellent combination. It does. If you don't have walnut oil, substitute 1½ teaspoons of dark sesame oil. ■ SERVES 4

2 large skinless, boneless chicken
    breasts, halved
250ml (8fl oz) Newman's Own Old-
    Fashioned Roadside Virgin
    Lemonade, or your favourite
15g (½oz) fresh breadcrumbs
25g (1oz) finely chopped pecans or
    walnuts

1 egg
5 tablespoons whole-grain mustard
vegetable oil for frying
3–4 teaspoons walnut oil
125ml (4fl oz) chicken stock
4 tablespoons double cream
salt and freshly ground black pepper to
    taste

Marinate the chicken in the lemonade for 1 hour. Drain, reserving the lemonade, and pat the chicken dry with kitchen paper.

Stir together the breadcrumbs and nuts on a plate. Put the egg in a shallow bowl and beat lightly. Place 3 tablespoons of the mustard in another bowl.

Brush the chicken with the mustard, dip into the beaten egg, then dredge in the crumbs and nuts. Chill, loosely covered, for 2–3 hours.

Heat 1cm (½in) of the vegetable oil with the walnut oil in a large frying pan until hot. Add the breaded chicken and fry, turning once, for 10–12 minutes. Transfer to a plate and keep warm.

While the chicken is cooking, combine the reserved lemonade, stock and the remaining 2 tablespoons of the mustard in a small saucepan. Bring to the boil and reduce over high heat to 125ml (4fl oz). Add the cream and cook for about 1½ minutes to heat through and thicken slightly. Season with salt and pepper, and pour over the chicken. Serve hot.

Caroline's Southern-Fried Chicken

Our housekeeper, Caroline Murphy, has taken several of the dishes she sets on our table and contributed them to this book. Her Ham Hocks and Beans (page 72) is one of my all-time favourites, her Tuna Salad is unmatched (page 115), and her southern-fried chicken is out of this world. ▓ **SERVES 2 TO 3**

1.5kg (3lb) chicken, cut up	herbamare or spike (see seasoning
sea salt	note)
paprika	475ml (16fl oz) vegetable oil

Season the chicken well with the sea salt, paprika and Herbamare. Refrigerate for 1 hour to let the seasonings penetrate the chicken.

Heat the oil in a frying pan until very hot and fry the chicken for 12–15 minutes on each side. Cover to prevent splattering and help the chicken cook faster.

NOTE: Spike seasoning is a mixture of assorted herbs and seaweed. It can be found in most health food stores.

Martha Stewart's Chicken Cataplana

A cataplana is a copper Portuguese cooking pan. If you don't have one, use a small casserole with a tight-fitting lid instead. This is a great one-dish meal, essentially a meat-and-potatoes combination, but it's light. ■ SERVES 4

2 tablespoons olive oil

350ml (12fl oz) Newman's Own All-Natural Bandito Salsa, or your favourite

2 medium potatoes, peeled and thinly sliced

2 skinless, boneless chicken breasts, halved

1 onion, thinly sliced

1 teaspoon dried oregano

salt and freshly ground black pepper to taste

Preheat the oven to 180°C, 350°F, gas mark 4.

Place the oil in the bottom of the cataplana or casserole. Add half of the salsa. Top with the sliced potatoes, chicken breasts, and onion. Top with the remaining salsa and sprinkle the oregano over it. Season with salt and pepper. Cover and bake for 1½ hours.

Chicken Cassidy Kebabs and the Sundance Orzo Pilaf

Aban Lal paired spiced chicken kebabs with a savoury pilaf studded with colourful fruits, vegetables and almonds, and enriched with cheese, to become a finalist in 1994. He donated his award to Habitat for Humanity and UNICEF. ■ SERVES 6

1kg (2lb) skinless, boneless chicken breasts, cut into 5cm (2in) cubes

MARINADE

250ml (8fl oz) Newman's Own Olive Oil and Vinegar Dressing, or your favourite

2 teaspoons root ginger, ground into a paste

2 teaspoons garlic paste

¾ teaspoon or less cayenne pepper

SUNDANCE ORZO PILAF

500g (1lb) freshly cooked orzo

250ml (8fl oz) Newman's Own Olive Oil and Vinegar Dressing, or your favourite

75ml (3fl oz) orange juice concentrate

4 tablespoons finely chopped mint

2 tablespoons or less red chilli oil

1 teaspoon finely chopped root ginger

50g (2oz) dried apricots, chopped

150g (5oz) currants

125g (4oz) toasted slivered almonds

125g (4oz) sun-dried tomatoes packed in oil, chopped

1 large green pepper, seeded and diced

125g (4oz) red onion, finely chopped

125g (4oz) goat's cheese, cubed (optional)

thin orange slices for garnish

mint sprigs for garnish

Place the chicken in a glass dish or bowl.

Mix the marinade ingredients together and pour over the chicken. Cover and refrigerate for at least 5 hours or overnight, turning occasionally.

Remove the chicken from the marinade and thread on 12 soaked wooden skewers.

To make the pilaf, place the orzo in a large bowl. In another bowl, whisk together the dressing, orange juice concentrate, mint, chilli oil and ginger. Pour the dressing over the orzo and mix well. Add the remaining ingredients and toss gently. Cover the bowl and keep at room temperature while the kebabs cook.

Light the barbecue. When ready to serve, grill the skewers for about 5–6 minutes on each side on the barbecue or under the grill.

Transfer the orzo to a serving dish. Arrange the cooked chicken skewers attractively on top. Garnish with the orange slices and mint sprigs.

Whenever I do something good, right away I've got to do something bad, so I know I'm not going to pieces.

—PAUL NEWMAN, 1985

Greek Chicken Oregano Afloat in the Diavolo Drowning Pool

Developing a recipe using Newman's Own All-Natural Diavolo Sauce was easy for Helen Conwell. She found that the spicy base blends perfectly with and enhances the flavours found in traditional Mediterranean cuisine. Helen, a 1995 finalist, donated her award to Ecumenical Ministries of the Eastern Shore Literacy Council. ■ SERVES 8

4 chicken breasts, halved
salt
1 large onion, sliced
1 garlic clove, finely chopped
2 tablespoons olive oil
one 800g (26oz) jar Newman's Own
    All-Natural Diavolo Sauce, or your
    favourite
1 bay leaf
2 tablespoons finely chopped fresh
    oregano, plus sprigs for garnish

1 tablespoon finely chopped fresh
    thyme
1 teaspoon ground cinnamon
one 300g (10oz) pack frozen artichoke
    hearts, cooked according to packet
    directions
1 tablespoon fresh lemon juice
½ teaspoon sugar
250g (8oz) orzo, cooked according to
    pack directions
1 tablespoon finely chopped parsley

Preheat the grill. Sprinkle the chicken with ½ teaspoon of salt. Grill the chicken, skin side up, 12–18cm (5–7in) from the heat until blistered and browned, about 10 minutes. Set aside.

Meanwhile, in a deep frying pan, sauté the onion and garlic in 1 tablespoon of the oil over medium heat until softened, about 10–12 minutes. Add the sauce, bay leaf, oregano, thyme and cinnamon. Scrape up any brown bits from the bottom of the frying pan.

Add the chicken, cover, and simmer for 30 minutes, turning once after 15 minutes, until the juices run clear. Add the artichoke hearts, lemon juice and sugar. Remove the chicken, place in a bowl, and keep warm.

Boil the sauce, uncovered, until it thickens and the artichoke hearts are heated through. Add salt to taste.

Toss the orzo with the parsley and the remaining 1 tablespoon of oil. Arrange the orzo on 2 sides of a serving platter. Arrange the chicken mixture in the middle and spoon the sauce over it. Garnish with the oregano sprigs.

Ismail Merchant's Yogurt Chicken
(Dahi Murgh) ■ SERVES 10 TO 12

125g (4fl oz) cup vegetable oil

2 onions, chopped

4 dried whole red chillies

12 cloves

2.75kg (5½lb) chicken drumsticks and
thighs

2.5cm (1in) piece of root ginger, peeled
and grated

350ml (12fl oz) plain yogurt

1 teaspoon salt

1 tablespoon freshly ground black
pepper

Heat the oil in a large heavy-bottomed frying pan or saucepan over medium heat. When hot, add the onions, chillies and cloves. Cook, stirring frequently, until the onions brown.

Add the chicken and ginger and stir continuously until the meat is seared on all sides.

Mix the yogurt with 250ml (8fl oz) of water. Add to the pan with the salt and pepper. Cover and cook over medium-low heat, stirring occasionally, for 1 hour.

Hotch Potch
You can actually throw anything that's handy into the pan, and it will fit right in with this dish. ■ SERVES 4

4 medium potatoes, peeled, quartered, and parboiled

3 tablespoons cooking oil

750g (1½lb) chicken breasts, skinned, boned, and cut into bite-sized pieces

40g (1½oz) butter or margarine

1 onion, coarsely chopped

1 stalk celery, coarsely chopped

1 green pepper, seeded and coarsely chopped

1 red pepper, seeded and coarsely chopped

2 tomatoes, peeled and chopped

pepper

Worcestershire sauce to taste

4 tablespoons soy sauce

In a heavy pan, brown the potatoes well in half of the oil. Remove and set aside. Brown the chicken pieces in the same pan, lower the heat, and continue cooking, stirring occasionally. While the chicken is cooking, prepare the vegetables.

In a separate pan set over medium-high heat, sauté the onion and celery in the butter until golden. Add the peppers and toss for about 1 minute. Add the tomatoes, pepper, Worcestershire sauce and soy sauce. Simmer for 1 to 2 minutes, add the chicken and potatoes, stir together, and serve.

Hotch's Chicken Marinara
The Italian-style stuffing of spinach and cheese is a savoury surprise in this easy-to-prepare dish.

▓ **SERVES 4**

2 large skinless, boneless chicken breasts, halved

50g (2oz) unsalted butter

1 small onion, diced

500g (1lb) fresh spinach or one 300g (10oz) pack frozen chopped spinach

50g (2oz) ricotta cheese

2 tablespoons freshly grated Parmesan cheese

⅛ teaspoon ground nutmeg

one 800g (26oz) jar Newman's Own All-Natural Spaghetti Sauce with Mushrooms, or your favourite

250g (8oz) spinach noodles or linguine

Preheat the oven to 180°C, 350°F, gas mark 4.

Form a pocket in the underside of each chicken breast, where the bone was removed, for the stuffing.

Heat 2 tablespoons of the butter in a saucepan. Add the onion and sauté until golden.

Wash the spinach if fresh, remove the stalks and cook in the water that clings to the leaves, about 2 minutes. Drain well and chop. If using frozen spinach, thaw and drain well. Combine with the onion in the pan. Remove from the heat and add the cheeses and nutmeg.

Stuff a few tablespoons of the mixture in each chicken breast. Fold the ends of the chicken under to enclose the filling. Spread the remaining butter on the bottom of a baking dish. Arrange the chicken pieces in the dish, stuffed side down. Pour the sauce over the chicken and bake for 45–50 minutes.

Cook the noodles and serve with the chicken breasts, spooning sauce over all.

Braised Chicken with 'Say Cheese' Pasta Sauce, Mushrooms and Walnuts

As executive chef and director of Manhattan's Rainbow Room complex, Waldy Malouf has the formidable challenge of overseeing pre-theatre, dinner, and late-night supper in the Rainbow Room, dinner and supper in the Rainbow and Stars cabaret, as well as the bar and Sunday brunch menus in the Promenade Bar.

Malouf also represents Rainbow's commitment to charity as a participating chef for Share Our Strength's Taste of the Nation. In addition, he represents Rainbow's commitment to hunger-relief causes and culinary education by volunteering his services at many events, including God's Love We Deliver, The Culinary Institute of America, Citymeals-on-Wheels, the James Beard House and Farmhands-Cityhands. ■ SERVES 4

8 chicken pieces, such as breasts, thighs or legs
coarse salt and freshly ground black pepper
flour for dredging
4 tablespoons vegetable oil
250g (8oz) mushrooms, quartered
125ml (4fl oz) dry white wine (optional)

one 800g (26oz) jar Newman's Own 'Say Cheese' Pasta Sauce, or your favourite

GARNISH

50g (2oz) chopped walnuts
2 tablespoons chopped fresh parsley or basil

Preheat the oven to 190°C, 375°F, gas mark 5.

Pat the chicken dry with kitchen paper, season with salt and pepper, and dredge in flour, shaking off the excess.

Heat the oil in a 30cm (12in) ovenproof frying pan. Add the chicken pieces, skin side down, and brown over medium heat for 7–8 minutes, until crisp and golden. Turn the chicken over and cook for 3–4 minutes more. Remove the chicken from the pan and set aside. Continue to cook the fat until the solids stick to the pan without burning and the fat is clear. Discard the fat, add the mushrooms, and cook for 3 minutes. Add the wine and bring to a simmer, stirring to incorporate the browned bits. Reduce by half. Add the sauce and bring to the boil. Return the chicken to the pan, skin side up.

Place the pan in the oven and bake the chicken, uncovered, for 10 minutes. Remove the breast pieces and keep warm. Cook the dark meat for 5 minutes more. Transfer the chicken to a serving casserole and pour the sauce over it. Sprinkle the walnuts and parsley on top.

You want to get a bead on a new restaurant? Order something you don't like. If you like it, you got a bead on a new restaurant.

—PAUL NEWMAN

Grilled Cumin Chicken Salad

If you make the dressing and bake the tortillas in advance, this is an easy salad to put together and great for hot weather get-togethers. You can also grill the chicken if it's too cold or inconvenient to use the barbecue. Try it with Joanne Woodward's Gazpacho (page 47). ■ MAKES ABOUT 350ML (12FL OZ) OF CUMIN DRESSING ■ SERVES 6

3 tablespoons ground cumin

3 tablespoons rapeseed oil

3 skinless, boneless chicken breasts

salt and freshly ground black pepper to taste

2 corn tortillas

olive oil

CUMIN DRESSING

4 tablespoons Dijon mustard

4 tablespoons distilled white vinegar

4 tablespoons fresh lemon juice

4 tablespoons ground cumin

1 tablespoon finely chopped shallot

175ml (6fl oz) rapeseed oil

½ teaspoon salt

1 tablespoon finely ground black pepper

SALAD

2 heads romaine or cos lettuce, chopped

2 plum tomatoes, diced

4 spring onions, thinly sliced

1 ripe avocado, peeled, stoned and diced

½ cucumber, diced

½ small red onion, cut into julienne strips

75g (3oz) chopped and pitted olives

To make the cumin dressing, in a bowl stir together the mustard, vinegar, lemon juice, cumin and shallot. Add the oil slowly, whisking it in until combined. Season with salt and pepper. Transfer the dressing to a covered container and refrigerate until ready to use.

In a shallow, flat dish, combine the cumin and oil. Add the chicken and turn to coat with the mixture. Season to taste with salt and pepper. Refrigerate while you prepare the tortillas and salad.

Preheat the oven to 190°C, 375°F, gas mark 5. Cut the tortillas into julienne strips and place on a baking sheet. Sprinkle the pieces very lightly with olive oil, salt and pepper. Bake, turning them, until golden brown, 5–10 minutes.

Combine the salad ingredients in a large serving bowl.

Light the barbecue and leave until hot.

Grill the chicken breasts for about 12 minutes on each side, turning them, until no longer pink inside. Transfer to a plate, allow to cool, then shred the chicken. Add to the salad.

Just before serving, add the tortillas to the salad with 175ml (6fl oz) of the dressing and toss. Serve with the remaining dressing on the side if desired.

Cassidy's Chicken Curry

Gloria Bradley of Naperville, Illinois, took Newman's Own on an exotic and flavourful trip through Southeast Asia, and discovered that the mild buttermilk flavour of Newman's Own Ranch Salad Dressing serves to accentuate the characteristic Asian flavours of coconut milk, curry powder, coconut, peanuts and fresh basil. Gloria, a 1995 finalist, donated her award to the Misericordia Home for Children. ■ SERVES 4

1 tablespoon olive oil
1 onion, chopped
2 garlic cloves, finely chopped
1 large red pepper, seeded and cut into thin strips
1 large green pepper, seeded and cut into thin strips
625g (1¼lb) skinless, boneless chicken breasts, cut into 2cm (¾in) pieces
2 tablespoons fresh lime juice
1 tablespoon curry powder

125ml (4fl oz) coconut milk (not cream of coconut)
125ml (4fl oz) Newman's Own Ranch Dressing, or your favourite
2 tablespoons chopped fresh basil or 2 teaspoons dried
½ teaspoon crushed red pepper flakes
500g (1lb) hot cooked rice
peanuts, chopped coriander and shredded coconut as toppings

Heat the oil in a 30cm (12in) nonstick frying pan over medium-high heat until hot. Add the onion and garlic and cook for 2 minutes. Add the peppers and cook, stirring, until lightly browned. Remove the mixture to a small bowl.

Add the chicken pieces to the frying pan with the lime juice, curry powder and 2 tablespoons of the coconut milk. Cook until the chicken loses its pink colour, about 4–5 minutes.

Stir in the remaining coconut milk, the dressing, basil and red pepper flakes. Add the pepper mixture and cook over medium heat for about 5 minutes, until heated through.

Serve the curry over the hot cooked rice with the toppings on the side.

Kiss of the Mediterranean Poussins

Lotte Mendelsohn, who hosts 'Dining Around with Lotte Mendelsohn' on WRKO radio in Boston and is food editor of TAB newspapers there, was the 1995 food pro finalist. She donated her award to the Boys and Girls Club of the Monterey Peninsula. Lotte recommends serving this over seasoned rice. ■ SERVES 4

2 large poussins, 750g–1kg (1½–2lb) each, halved
salt and freshly ground black pepper to taste
3 tablespoons virgin olive oil
2 garlic cloves, halved
1 rounded teaspoon ground cinnamon
¼ teaspoon ground cloves

3 tablespoons balsamic vinegar
60g (2½oz) blanched almonds
2 tablespoons fresh basil
one 425g (14oz) jar Newman's Own Bombolina Spaghetti Sauce, or your favourite
lemon zest curls for garnish

Preheat the oven to 220°C, 425°F, gas mark 7.

Rinse and pat the poussins dry with kitchen paper. Lightly salt and pepper the insides.

Heat the oil in a shallow roasting tin. Lightly brown the garlic, but do not let it burn. Remove and discard the garlic. Add the poussins to the garlic oil and brown on both sides. Pour off the excess oil and fat in the tinn and arrange the poussins skin side down.

Make a paste with the cinnamon, cloves and 2 tablespoons of the vinegar. Brush half of it over the poussins. Place in the oven and bake for 10 minutes. Turn the poussins and brush with the remaining spice paste. Bake for 10 minutes more.

Meanwhile, in a mini-mixer or blender, coarsely grind the almonds. Add the basil leaves and process until the mixture has the consistency of coarse sand. In a bowl, blend the remaining 1 tablespoon of vinegar with the almond mixture and sauce.

Pour the sauce over the poussins, brushing some of it on the undersides. Bake, skin side up, for 10–15 minutes, or until the almond paste bubbles slightly.

Serve garnished with the lemon zest curls.

Incredible Cobb Salad

This variation of the classic lunch salad includes most of the expected ingredients in the traditional recipe, plus some dandy surprises. Toss well with a judicious amount of dressing and have extra on the side. You can also serve this in hollowed-out whole-grain rolls.

The yolks of the six hard-boiled eggs don't make an appearance in this updated version. If you want, do include them. ▪ MAKES ABOUT 475ML (16FL OZ) OF DRESSING ▪ SERVES 6

2 tablespoons olive oil
1 small courgette, diced
1 small red pepper, seeded and diced
1 small yellow pepper, seeded and diced
1 Japanese or small aubergine, diced
salt and freshly ground black pepper to taste
3 skinless, boneless chicken breast halves, cooked and cut into cubes
6 slices bacon, cooked and diced
6 hard-boiled eggs, peeled, yolks removed and the whites chopped
1 small head Chinese cabbage, shredded

2 avocados, peeled, stoned and diced
50g (2oz) French blue cheese, crumbled

DRESSING

75g (3oz) French blue cheese, crumbled
2 tablespoons Dijon mustard
1 teaspoon very finely chopped garlic
75ml (3fl oz) fresh lemon juice
1 teaspoon Worcestershire sauce
75ml (3fl oz) distilled white vinegar
250ml (8fl oz) vegetable oil
½ teaspoon salt
1 teaspoon freshly ground black pepper

To make the dressing, combine half the blue cheese, the mustard, garlic, lemon juice, Worcestershire sauce and vinegar in a food processor and blend. The mixture will be thick. Add the oil in a thin, steady stream and 75ml (3fl oz) of water. Blend until smooth. Add the salt and pepper, and blend for 10 seconds more. Pour the dressing into a bowl and stir in the remaining blue cheese. Cover and leave to stand for 1 hour at room temperature before serving.

Heat the oil in a large frying pan over high heat until hot. Add the courgette, peppers and aubergine and sauté, tossing. Add 4 tablespoons of water and cook for 6 minutes, until tender but still crisp. Season lightly with salt and pepper. Drain off any remaining liquid and transfer to a large mixing bowl to cool.

Add the chicken, bacon, chopped egg whites, cabbage, avocados and blue cheese to the sautéed vegetables and toss well. Pour on the dressing to taste and toss again. Serve the remaining dressing in a bowl on the side.

There are three rules for running a business. Fortunately, we don't know any of them.

—A. E. HOTCHNER TO PAUL NEWMAN
AS THEY SENT 804,000 CONTAINERS
OF LEMONADE TO THE TROOPS IN
DESERT STORM

Spice-Rubbed Roasted Turkey Breast

This herb-and-spice-coated turkey breast goes very well with Creamy Potato Salad (page 168). If you're thinking of making a picnic of this—and this makes good picnic food—double the salad. The garlic granules are available at most supermarkets.

■ SERVES 8 TO 10

1 boneless turkey breast, about
   2–2.5kg (4–4½lb)
buttermilk for soaking the turkey
   breast

SPICE RUB

4 tablespoons cumin seeds
4 tablespoons dried rosemary

4 tablespoons garlic granules
4 tablespoons dried parsley
1 teaspoon salt
1 tablespoon freshly ground black
   pepper
1 tablespoon olive oil

The day before you plan to cook the turkey breast, put it in a bowl and pour on enough buttermilk to cover it. Cover the bowl, and place in the refrigerator overnight.

The next day, preheat the oven to 230°C, 450°F, gas mark 8.

In a small bowl, toss all the spice rub ingredients together.

Remove the turkey breast from the buttermilk, letting the milk drip off. Pat the spice rub evenly all over the turkey breast, pressing it on. Place in a small baking tin and cover the tin with foil.

Cook in the oven for 35 minutes. Lower the temperature to 190°C, 375°F, gas mark 5, remove the foil and cook for another 25 minutes, until nicely browned.

Remove the turkey breast from the oven and place on a cutting board. Leave to cool, then cut into thin slices.

The Grilled Bird of Youth Meets Judge Roy Bean Salad

Doyle Haeussler was motivated at an early age to be highly creative with fowl: while growing up, there was an overabundance of it in her parents' freezer! Newman's Own Olive Oil and Vinegar Salad Dressing is the secret ingredient in her recipe of grilled duck breast served over a salad of cannellini beans. Doyle, a 1995 grand prize-winner, donated her award to the Special Olympics of Indiana, the US Holocaust Memorial Museum and the Community Association of Muncie and Delaware Counties. ■ SERVES 4

2 boneless duck breasts, halved, or
    2 skinless, boneless chicken
    breasts, halved
250ml (8fl oz) Newman's Own Olive Oil
    and Vinegar Dressing, or your
    favourite
250g (8oz) mixed salad greens
two 575g (19oz) cans cannellini beans,
    rinsed and drained
2 spring onions, chopped

4 tablespoons finely chopped flat-leaf
    parsley
2 tablespoons finely chopped basil
600ml (1 pint) red and/or yellow
    cherry tomatoes, halved
1 red pepper, seeded and cut into thin
    strips
1 yellow bell pepper, seeded and cut
    into thin strips

Place the duck in a bowl with 125ml (4fl oz) of the dressing. Cover and refrigerate overnight.

Light the barbecue.

Drain the duck, discarding the marinade, and pat dry with kitchen paper. Grill the duck over medium heat, preferably over aromatic wood, until it is no longer pink inside when cut and the skin is crisp and browned. Alternatively, grill the duck under a preheated grill for 7–8 minutes. (If using chicken, grill until the meat is no longer pink inside when cut, about 4 minutes on each side.)

Divide the salad greens between 4 dinner plates. Toss the cannellini beans with the remaining dressing, the onions, parsley and basil. Top the greens with the bean mixture. Arrange some tomato halves and pepper strips around the plate. Slice the duck breasts on the diagonal and lay the slices over the top of the salads. Serve with additional dressing if desired.

Joanne Woodward's Sole Cabernet This is at the top of my list of favourite dishes. It is in a class by itself. ■ SERVES 4

50g (2oz) unsalted butter

4 fillets of sole, 1–1.25kg (2–2½lb)

salt and freshly ground black pepper to taste

2 shallots, chopped

475ml (16fl oz) good cabernet sauvignon

250ml (8fl oz) Joanne's Hollandaise Sauce (recipe follows)

Preheat the oven to 190°C, 375°F, gas mark 5.

Put dabs of butter on the fillets of sole and fold them over crosswise. Add the salt, pepper, and shallots. Place the fillets in a baking tin and add the cabernet sauvignon. Bake for 10 minutes, then transfer the fish to a plate with a slotted spoon.

Pour the wine sauce into a saucepan and reduce to ⅓ the original amount. Leave to cool. Stir Joanne's Hollandaise Sauce into the wine sauce. Return the sole and sauce to the baking tin. Place in the oven for 5 minutes before serving.

Joanne's Hollandaise Sauce

3 egg yolks
3 tablespoons cold water
125g (4oz) lightly salted butter, melted

freshly ground pepper to taste
juice of ½ lemon

Place the egg yolks and water in the top of a double boiler over hot but not boiling water. Whisk rapidly until the mixture thickens and leaves a trail. Remove from the heat. Add the butter, little by little, while continuing to whisk. Add the pepper. Add the lemon juice just before serving.

Dilled Fillets of Cod à la Newman

Coming in a distant second to Joanne's Sole Cabernet is my own dilled fillet of cod, which I bake in the oven, liberally coating it with lots of fresh dill, butter and lemon juice.

■ SERVES 4

1kg (2lb) young cod fillets
3–4 tablespoons chopped fresh dill or
   1 tablespoon dried
125g (4oz) unsalted butter

175ml (6fl oz) dry white wine
250ml (8fl oz) Joanne's Hollandaise
   Sauce (page 103)

Preheat the oven to 190°C, 375°F, gas mark 5.

Wash the fillets and pat dry with kitchen paper. Arrange in a single layer in a 32 x 23 x 5cm (13 x 9 x 2in) baking dish. Cover with the dill. Heat the butter and wine together in a small saucepan until the butter melts. Pour over the fish. Bake for 20 minutes, or just until the fish separates easily when touched with a fork.

Serve with Joanne's Hollandaise Sauce.

Italian Baked Cod

This is really a variation on Dilled Fillets of Cod (page 104), but the resulting flavour is so different that it deserves a page of its own. The amount of onions, tomatoes and olives is entirely up to you.

SERVES 4

1kg (2lb) young cod fillets
salt and freshly ground black pepper to taste
sliced onions
tomatoes, chopped and stewed
ripe olives, stoned and sliced

2 tablespoons chopped fresh basil or 1 tablespoon dried
2 tablespoons chopped fresh parsley or 1 tablespoon dried
1 garlic clove, crushed
clam juice

Preheat the oven to 190°C, 375°F, gas mark 5.

Wash the fillets and pat dry with kitchen paper. Arrange in a single layer in a 32 x 23 x 5cm (13 x 9 x 2in) baking dish. Season with salt and pepper. Cover with the onions, tomatoes, olives, basil, parsley and garlic. Moisten with a little clam juice.

Bake for 20 minutes, or just until the fish separates easily when touched with a fork. Drain off most of the liquid before serving.

Mediterranean Fish Fillets
Up the ante here by stirring a little pesto into basmati rice to serve with these easy-to-make, quick-cooking fillets. The black olive paste is available in jars at the supermarket. ■ SERVES 4

2 tablespoons black olive paste

1 tablespoon Dijon mustard

4 red snapper or flounder fillets, about 1kg (2lb)

125ml (4fl oz) Newman's Own Bombolina Spaghetti Sauce, or your favourite

4 sun-dried tomatoes in oil, cut into thin strips

2 teaspoons fresh lemon juice

½ teaspoon grated lemon zest

25g (1oz) slivered almonds, toasted

shredded fresh basil leaves for garnish

grated lemon zest for garnish

Combine the olive paste and mustard in a small bowl.

Preheat the oven to 240°C, 475°F, gas mark 9. Coat a baking sheet with oil.

Fold the ends of each fillet under to form a square, then spread some of the olive paste mixture on top. Arrange the squares on the prepared baking sheet and bake for 12–15 minutes, or until the fish separates easily when touched with a fork.

Meanwhile, in a small saucepan, heat the sauce with the tomatoes, lemon juice and zest over medium heat until hot.

When the fillets are done, transfer to plates and spoon some of the hot sauce on top. Garnish with the almonds, basil and lemon zest. Serve at once.

Herbed Salmon Fillets in Foil

These parcels make entertaining very easy because they can be prepared entirely in advance—first thing in the morning, if you like—and kept in the refrigerator until cooking time. Just as important, they take only twelve minutes to cook. Serve with Balsamic Aubergine and Potatoes (page 163) for a dynamite combination. ▦ SERVES 6

six 175g (6oz) salmon fillets
salt and freshly ground black pepper to
   taste
6 thin lemon slices
250ml (8fl oz) Newman's Own Caesar
   Dressing, or your favourite

8 garlic cloves, chopped
1 tablespoon chopped fresh thyme
3 handfuls whole-wheat croûtons

Preheat the oven to 230°C, 450°F, gas mark 8. Have ready 6 pieces of foil, large enough to enclose 1 fillet.

Place a fillet in the middle of a piece of foil. Season with salt and pepper, and put a lemon slice on top. Pour 2½ tablespoons of dressing over each fillet. Sprinkle with the garlic and thyme and scatter some croûtons over each fillet. Enclose in the foil, sealing it airtight and leaving a little space at the top for the parcel to expand.

Bake the parcels on the rack of the oven for 12 minutes. (The parcels will puff up slightly.) Transfer the parcels to dinner plates. Open them carefully because there is a build-up of steam inside.

Salmon Supper Salad

You can serve these salads for either lunch or supper, along with soup to round out the meal, or as a very appealing, substantial first course of a simplified dinner menu. You will have leftover dressing. It's good on almost any kind of salad. **MAKES 250ML (8FL OZ) OF DRESSING** **SERVES 6**

DRESSING

4 tablespoons balsamic vinegar
4 tablespoons fresh lime juice
2 tablespoons Dijon mustard
4 tab;espoons chopped chives
1 shallot, chopped
1 teaspoon ground cumin
125ml (4fl oz) olive oil
salt and freshly ground black pepper to taste

500g (1lb) mixed baby greens
2 tomatoes, chopped
1 bunch spring onions, thinly sliced
½ small red onion, thinly sliced
1½ avocados, peeled, stoned and diced
three 175–200g (6–7oz) salmon fillets
olive oil for brushing the salmon
salt and freshly ground black pepper to taste

To make the dressing, combine the vinegar, lime juice, mustard, chives, shallot and cumin in a blender or food processor and blend until combined. With the motor running, add the oil in a slow, steady stream, blending until emulsified. Season with salt and pepper. Transfer the dressing to a container and let stand for 1 hour at room temperature before serving.

Light the barbecue.

In a large bowl, combine the greens, tomatoes, spring onions, red onion and avocados.

Brush the salmon fillets with the oil on both sides and arrange in a hinged grill basket. Grill for 6–8 minutes on each side, depending on the thickness. (You can also cook the fillets in a preheated grill pan on the top of the stove for the same amount of time per side.) Let the salmon fillets cool, then remove the skin. Crumble the salmon into bite-sized chunks and add to the salad with 75ml (3fl oz) of the dressing. Toss gently and add salt and pepper. Serve with additional dressing on the side if desired.

Dear Mr. Newman:

I wish to commend and compliment you on the excellence and versatility of your salad dressing, Newman's Own Oil and Vinegar Dressing. . . . The other day I took a walk on the beach during my lunch hour, which is how I normally spend my lunches. This was preceded by a light but satisfying meal of a green salad topped by Newman's Own Olive Oil and Vinegar Salad Dressing. As I was saying, I took a walk on the beach, in the fine City of Solana Beach, and the only proper way to walk on the beach is to go barefoot. . . .

When I got back to work, still barefoot, I noticed a large patch of tar which I had apparently stepped in while walking. . . . Well, Mr. Newman (may I call you Paul?), I remembered my lunch and your fine-tasting oil and vinegar dressing—and you know what, it really did the trick! Two applications of Newman's Own to the bottom of my foot really cut through the grease and grime and took that tar patch right off, baby. Not only is your product a treat for the palate, but it's also a great cleaning agent—and biodegradable, too—truly a product for all seasons. . . .

MOST SINCERELY,
K.J.

Hotchner's Spanish Swordfish

Hemingway and I used to eat at a little restaurant on the beach at Torremolinas in southernmost Spain, run by an old Basque fisherman. We were so smitten by this swordfish that I asked the old man to show me how to cook it. I once tried to cook it on a barbecue in Ketchum, Idaho, but the swordfish was frozen and had no taste. Now I often show it off in Connecticut when the local fish store alerts me to a swordfish fresh off the hook.

Make sure the pine bough you use has not been sprayed with pesticides. Rinse and dry it well before using. ▪ SERVES 4 TO 6

1kg (2lb) swordfish steak, 5cm (2 in) thick and cut evenly
250ml (8fl oz) Newman's Own Salad Dressing, Newman's Vinaigrette Dressing (page 30), or your favourite
4 tablespoons fresh lime juice

3 tablespoons fresh thyme or rosemary, or 1 tablespoon dried plus additional for cooking
lemon juice
butter
1 small freshly cut pine bough

Marinate the swordfish in the salad dressing, lime juice and thyme or rosemary for several hours in the refrigerator.

Light the barbecue and place the fish on the grill when the coals are grey. Saturate with lemon juice, chunks of butter, and more thyme. Cook for 10 minutes on each side, turning only once. Baste with more lemon juice and marinade, and dot with butter after turning. Remove the fish, place the pine bough on the fire, put the fish on top, and let it be seared by the flame. Remove after the pine flame dies down and serve immediately.

Walter Bridge's Grilled Swordfish Steaks

Paul Newman's starring role as Walter Bridge (who loved to spark up the grill!) inspired Cynthia Mitchell to develop this hassle-free swordfish recipe. Fresh from the fisherman's net, the swordfish is marinated and basted with a wine-laced sauce of Newman's Own Ranch Dressing, fresh herbs, citrus juices and capers. The secret lies in the simplicity of preparation. Cynthia, a 1996 runner-up, donated her award to Friends of Homeless Animals. ■ **SERVES 4**

one 250g (8oz) bottle Newman's Own
    Ranch Dressing, or your favourite
4 tablespoons dry white wine
2 tablespoons fresh lemon juice
2 tablespoons fresh lime juice
1 tablespoon chopped fresh rosemary

1 tablespoon chopped fresh dill
1 tablespoon finely chopped capers
two 375g (12oz) swordfish steaks,
    2.5cm (1in) thick
lemon and lime slices for garnish
rosemary sprigs for garnish

In a 32 x 23cm (13 x 9in) baking dish, stir the dressing, white wine, lemon juice, lime juice, rosemary, dill and capers together until blended. Cut the swordfish steaks crosswise in half and add to the marinade, turning to coat them. Cover and refrigerate for at least 1 hour, turning occasionally.

Preheat the grill.

Remove the swordfish steaks, reserving the marinade, and place on a rack in a grill pan. Grill as close to the heat source as possible for 8–10 minutes without turning, until the fish flakes easily when tested with a fork. Brush once halfway through the grill time with some of the reserved marinade. Discard the remaining marinade.

(You can also barbecue the swordfish. About 45 minutes in advance of serving, light the barbecue. Grill the swordfish over medium heat for approximately 5 minutes on each side side. Brush once halfway through the grilling with the reserved marinade. The fish is done when it flakes easily when tested with a fork. Discard the remaining marinade.)

Place the swordfish on a platter and garnish with the lemon and lime slices and rosemary sprigs.

James Naughton's Honey Mustard Peppered Tuna Steaks

This seared fresh tuna on a bed of lightly seasoned cucumber and tomato salad is cooked until barely warm. It is meant to be very rare inside, so if you don't like rare tuna, this dish is not for you. You can substitute halibut or cod, however, and cook them until opaque throughout.

If you're a tuna lover, you will need the freshest, best-quality tuna you can lay your hands on. First choice is ahi ahi, which is also the most expensive and may not always be available. Second would be yellowfin. Securing the tuna, we'd wager, will be the most time-consuming part of making this stylish dish. You could also serve this in smaller portions as a first course at a dinner party.

■ MAKES 250ML (8FL OZ) OF DRESSING ■ SERVES 6

SALAD

625g (1¼lb) chopped tomatoes
300g (10oz) cucumber, cut into matchstick slices
2 tablespoons olive oil
2 tablespoons seasoned rice vinegar
salt and freshly ground black pepper to taste

DRESSING

125ml (4fl oz) tamari sauce
4 tablespoons seasoned rice vinegar
2 tablespoons Chinese hot mustard
2 tablespoons fresh lemon juice
1 tablespoon finely chopped basil
1 tablespoon finely chopped shallots
1 teaspoon finely chopped root ginger

TUNA

175ml (6fl oz) honey mustard
salt to taste
2 tablespoons coarsely ground black pepper
six 175–200g (6–7oz) tuna steaks, 2.5cm (1in) thick, or halibut or cod steaks

toasted sesame seeds for garnish (optional)

To make the salad, toss together all the ingredients in a bowl. Leave to stand at room temperature for 1 hour before serving.

To make the dressing, in another bowl, whisk all the ingredients together well.

Preheat the grill.

To prepare the fish, in a small bowl combine the mustard, salt and pepper. Place the fish on a baking sheet and generously brush on one side only with the mustard mixture. Place on the lowest rack and grill for 4–6 minutes without turning. (If using halibut or cod, grill for 5–8 minutes without turning.)

To serve, divide the salad among 6 plates and top with the fish. Spoon 3 tablespoons of dressing over the fish and serve the remaining dressing on the side. Garnish with the toasted sesame seeds.

James Naughton and Julia Roberts cavorting at the 1997 camp gala

The Hustler's Grilled Tuna Steaks with Caponata Relish

Rachel Sancilio of Virginia Beach, Virginia, loves to cook for her children and grandchildren. Her caponata, which can be made ahead of time, is a sure bet and a crowd pleaser. Rachel, a 1996 runner-up, donated her award to the Children's Hospital of the King's Daughters at Johns Hopkins Hospital. ■ SERVES 8

3 celery sticks, cut into 1cm (½in) pieces

2 onions, cut into 1cm (½in) pieces

3 tablespoons olive oil

salt

750g (1½lb) aubergine, cut into 1cm (½in) pieces

1 cup Newman's Own Bombolina Spaghetti Sauce, or your favourite

125ml (4fl oz) white wine vinegar

75g (3oz) ripe olives, stoned and sliced

75g (3oz) green olives, stoned and sliced

50g (2oz) sugar

2 tablespoons capers, drained

½ teaspoon dried basil

¼ teaspoon crushed red pepper flakes

freshly ground black pepper

eight 175g (6oz) tuna steaks, 2.5cm (1in) thick

25g (1oz) pine nuts, toasted, for garnish

Preheat the oven to 220°C, 425°F, gas mark 7.

Toss the celery and onions together in a roasting tin with 1 tablespoon of the oil and ¼ teaspoon of salt. In another roasting tin, toss the aubergine with the remaining 2 tablespoons of oil and ¼ teaspoon of salt. Put the tins in the oven on 2 different racks and roast the vegetables for 20 minutes, tossing them once halfway through the roasting time.

Combine all the roasted vegetables in a large roasting tin. Add the sauce, vinegar, olives, sugar, capers, basil, red pepper flakes and ¼ teaspoon of black pepper. Toss to mix well. Cover the pan with foil and bake in the oven for 30 minutes. Remove and keep warm.

Preheat the grill. Place the tuna steaks on a rack in the grill pan and sprinkle lightly on both sides with salt and black pepper. Grill as close to the heat source as possible for 4–5 minutes for rare, 10 minutes for well done, or until opaque throughout.

Serve the caponata, garnished with pine nuts, alongside the tuna steaks.

Caroline Murphy's Tuna Salad
This is another one of my favourites and just one of our housekeeper's triumphs. I like it as a sandwich on Nell's Sesame Loaves (page 180). ■ SERVES 2 TO 3

one 180g (6½oz) can tuna	3 tablespoons mayonnaise
1 teaspoon mustard	3 spring onions, finely chopped
1 whole sweet pickle, finely chopped	1 tablespoon sweet pickle juice

Drain the tuna and flake into a bowl. Add the remaining ingredients and mix well. Serve as a salad or sandwich filling.

Diavolo Seafood Loaves

Christine Loughridge showcases two of the finest products of the Pacific Northwest—sourdough bread and seafood—in her 1991 winning recipe. She donated her award to the Crohn's and Colitis Foundation of America. ■ SERVES 4

500–750g (1–1½lb) fresh seafood (red snapper, prawns, or whatever is available)

4 loaves sourdough bread, each about 12cm (5in) long

olive oil or a mixture of butter and oil

3 garlic cloves, chopped

2 spring onions, chopped

250ml (8fl oz) dry white wine

1 small red pepper, seeded and diced

1 small yellow pepper, seeded and diced

1 small green pepper, seeded and diced

one 800g (26oz) jar Newman's Own All-Natural Diavolo Sauce, or your favourite

1 bunch coriander, chopped, with 8 sprigs reserved for garnish

softened butter

tomato slices and orange slices for garnish

Preheat the oven to 200°C, 400°F, gas mark 6.

Clean or shell the seafood. Slice the top off each loaf, then hollow out the loaf to within 2.5cm (1in) of the sides. Cut the bread into cubes and put in a bowl. Drizzle with a little oil and ⅓ of the garlic and toss. Bake the croûtons on a baking sheet, tossing once, for 10 minutes, or until golden brown.

Heat 3 tablespoons of oil in a frying pan. Add another ⅓ of the garlic and the spring onions, and sauté over medium heat until the spring onions are softened. Add the wine and reduce by half. Add the seafood and peppers and sauté, stirring, just until the seafood is no longer transparent. Do not overcook. Remove the pan from the heat.

In a saucepan, heat the sauce and stir in the chopped coriander.

Preheat the grill.

Spread the softened butter on the inside of each hollowed-out loaf and sprinkle with the remaining garlic. Put the loaves under the grill to brown lightly.

To assemble, put ¼ of the seafood mixture into each loaf and add ¼ of the sauce, filling to within 2.5cm (1in) of the top. Sprinkle with the croûtons, garnish with the coriander sprigs, and lean the top of the loaf alongside. Fill the remaining loaves in the same way.

To serve, arrange the seafood loaves on a platter and garnish with the tomato and orange slices.

Garlic-Herb Marinated Halibut with Lemon

Sauce
If you want to go all out, serve the halibut on a bed of Garlicky Mashed Potatoes (page 164), with a sauté of mangetout, carrots and red onion on the side. The lemon sauce is good on almost anything. When it comes to seasoning the fish, though, only fresh herbs as a crust will do.

SERVES 6

6 Alaskan halibut steaks, about 200g (7oz) each	**LEMON SAUCE**
	90g (3½oz) unsalted butter, diced
40g (1½oz) chopped mixed fresh herbs, such as basil, parsley, coriander and tarragon	1 tablespoon chopped garlic
	125ml (4fl oz) dry white wine
	4 tablespoons fresh lemon juice
1 tablespoon finely chopped garlic	1 tablespoon soy sauce
4 tablespoons olive oil	salt and freshly ground black pepper to taste

Combine the herbs, garlic and oil in a shallow baking dish large enough to hold the halibut in 1 layer. Add the halibut steaks and turn to coat them on both sides with the herb mixture. Cover and refrigerate for 1 hour before cooking.

Preheat the grill.

Meanwhile, make the lemon sauce. In an enamel saucepan, melt 15g (½oz) of the butter over medium heat. Add the garlic and cook, stirring, until golden. Stir in the wine, lemon juice and soy sauce, and reduce the liquid by ⅓. Add the remaining butter, 1 piece at a time, quickly whisking until completely incorporated. Fully blend each piece, not just melt it, before adding the next. Taste and add salt and pepper. Keep the sauce warm in a bain-marie until ready to use. Do not reheat the sauce over direct heat.

Grill the halibut in the grill pan on the middle rack for about 6–8 minutes, or until just cooked through and the juices run clear when tested with a fork. (You can also roast it in a preheated 240°C, 475°F, gas mark 9 oven for 8–10 minutes without turning.)

Serve the halibut with several tablespoons of the lemon sauce drizzled over the top.

Sarah Jessica Parker's Grilled Prawns with Vodka-Lime Sauce

If you serve these prawns with Honey Mustard Mashed Potatoes (page 165), they are even better. Arrange the prawns, tails up, in a mound of potatoes, then drizzle on the sauce. There is something really fine in the way the mustard in the potatoes and the lime in the sauce intermingle. ■ MAKES ABOUT 175ML (6FL OZ) OF SAUCE ■ SERVES 6

36 extra-large raw prawns, peeled and
   deveined but with tails on
2 tablespoons olive oil
salt and freshly ground black pepper to
   taste
sliced spring onions, green and white
   parts, for garnish

VODKA-LIME SAUCE

250ml (8fl oz) vodka
250ml (8fl oz) dry white wine
75ml (3fl oz) fresh lime juice
175g (6oz) cold unsalted butter, diced
salt and freshly ground black pepper to
   taste

In a shallow flat-bottomed dish, combine the prawns with the oil, salt and pepper. Leave to stand at room temperature while preheating the barbecue.

Light the barbecue.

To make the vodka-lime sauce, combine the vodka, wine and lime juice in an enamel or glass saucepan. Reduce the mixture over medium heat to ⅓ the original amount. Add the butter, 1 piece at a time, quickly whisking in until completely incorporated. Blend each piece of butter in fully, not just melt it, before adding the next. Work quickly but do not increase the heat under the pan. Season with salt and pepper. Keep the sauce warm in a bain-marie until ready to use. Do not reheat the sauce over direct heat.

Arrange the prawns in 1 layer in a hinged grill basket. Grill over hot coals for 4 minutes on each side, or until just cooked through. You can also sauté them in batches, using 1 tablespoon of olive oil per batch, in a hot cast-iron fsrying pan for 4 minutes on each side.

To serve, put 5 prawns on each plate, spoon 2–3 tablespoons of sauce over them, and sprinkle spring onion rings on top. Serve at once.

Tasty Thai Prawns and Sesame Noodles

Exotic flavourings reminiscent of Far East cuisine blend together with Newman's Own Light Italian Dressing in a light, fast and easy Asian dish created by Beverly Ann Crummey of Brooksville, Florida. Now this restaurant favourite and 1993 grand prize winner can be enjoyed at home, week in and week out. Beverly Ann donated her award to Daystar Life Center. ■ **SERVES 4**

500g (1lb) raw prawns, peeled and deveined
one 250g (8oz) bottle Newman's Own Light Italian Dressing, or your favourite
2 tablespoons chunky peanut butter
1 tablespoon soy sauce
1 tablespoon honey
1 teaspoon grated peeled root ginger

½ teaspoon crushed red pepper flakes
250g (8oz) cappellini or angel hair pasta
2 tablespoons vegetable oil
1 tablespoon sesame oil
1 carrot, peeled and shredded
4 spring onions, chopped
2 tablespoons chopped coriander for garnish

In a medium bowl, mix the prawns with 75ml (3fl oz) of the dressing. Cover and refrigerate for 1 hour.

In a small bowl, whisk together the peanut butter, soy sauce, honey, ginger, red pepper flakes and the remaining dressing.

Drain the prawns and discard the marinade. Bring a large pan of salted water to the boil, add the pasta, and cook according to the package directions until firm but tender.

Meanwhile, in a large saucepan, heat the vegetable oil and sesame oil over high heat until very hot. Add the carrot and cook for 1 minute. Add the drained prawns and spring onions and cook, stirring constantly, for about 3 minutes, or until the prawns are opaque throughout.

Drain the pasta, place in a large bowl, and add the peanut sauce and prawn mixture. Toss to combine. Garnish with the chopped coriander and serve.

Piquant Scallops with Tangerines

The scallops 'cook' here first in vinegar, then in a lemony, gingery marinade. Try this for lunch on a hot summer day, when light eating is in order. Or halve the portions and serve it as an appetizer. Serve with chilled crisp white wine as an accompaniment. ▨ SERVES 4

375g (12oz) scallops, cut into quarters if large	1½ teaspoons finely chopped peeled root ginger
175ml (6fl oz) cider vinegar	pinch of cayenne pepper
75ml (3fl oz) Newman's Own Old-Fashioned Roadside Virgin Lemonade, or your favourite	salt and freshly ground black pepper to taste
1 tablespoon honey	1 head radicchio, finely shredded
1½ teaspoons walnut oil	whole coriander sprigs to taste
2 tablespoons finely diced green pepper	2–3 tangerines, peeled and membranes removed
½ garlic clove, finely chopped	1 tablespoon chopped chives (optional)

Place the scallops in a ceramic or glass bowl with the vinegar. Cover and marinate in the refrigerator for 1 hour. Drain and discard the vinegar. Rinse the scallops under cold running water and drain well.

In another glass bowl, combine the scallops with the lemonade, honey, oil, green pepper, garlic, ginger, cayenne pepper, salt and pepper. Toss, cover and marinate in the refrigerator, stirring occasionally, for 1½ hours.

Make a bed of shredded radicchio on each of 4 plates and add coriander sprigs. Divide the scallops among the plates and arrange tangerine sections around the sides. Drizzle with the marinade and sprinkle with chives. Serve chilled.

Joanne Woodward's Cioppino

Serve with crusty Italian bread. To round out the meal, add a salad of crisp lettuce with slivers of cheese and walnuts, tossed with your favourite vinaigrette. ▧ **SERVES 6**

4 tablespoons vegetable or olive oil

2 garlic cloves, finely chopped

2 onions, chopped

2 green peppers, seeded and chopped

one 800g (26oz) jar Newman's Own
    All-Natural Marinara Style
    Venetian Spaghetti Sauce, or your
    favourite

250ml (8fl oz) dry white wine

750g (1½lb) cod, sliced and cut into
    pieces

250g (8oz) frozen lobster tails, shelled
    and cut up

500g (1lb) mussels and/or small clams

Heat the oil in a deep, heavy frying pan or cassserole dish. Add the garlic, onions and peppers and cook until the onions are golden. Add the marinara sauce, wine, cod and lobster, and simmer for 6 minutes. Add the mussels, cover and cook for 5 minutes more, until the fish is done and the mussels have opened.

Blaze's Prawn and Sausage Creole

Sergeant Mark Maki finds cooking and experimenting with different cuisines great stress therapy. Inspired by Cajun cooking, Mark created a quick and easy Creole recipe—a hassle-free dinner for any day of the week. He donated the money from his 1995 grand prize to Covenant Christian School. ■ SERVES 6

25g (1oz) unsalted butter or margarine

2 celery stalks, chopped

1 yellow pepper, seeded and chopped

1 large onion, chopped

375g (12oz) kielbasa, sliced

1 garlic clove, finely chopped

350ml (12fl oz) clam juice

250ml (8fl oz) Newman's Own
    Bombolina Spaghetti Sauce, or
    your favourite

500g (1lb) raw prawns, peeled and
    deveined

500g (1lb) hot cooked rice

SPICE MIXTURE

1 bay leaf

½ teaspoon dried thyme

½ teaspoon dried basil

½ teaspoon salt

½ teaspoon white pepper

¼ teaspoon cayenne pepper

¼ teaspoon freshly ground black
    pepper

In a 30cm (12in) frying pan, heat the butter or margarine over medium-high heat until hot. Add the celery and pepper and sauté for 8–10 minutes, until softened. Remove the mixture from the pan and set aside. Add the onion and kielbasa to the frying pan and sauté for 10 minutes. Stir in the garlic and cook for 30 seconds.

Add the clam juice, sauce, and all the spice mixture ingredients, and bring to the boil. Cover and simmer for 5 minutes. Add the prawns and cook for 2–3 minutes, until the prawns turn opaque throughout. Add the reserved celery mixture and heat through. Remove the bay leaf.

To serve, spoon the hot rice into large shallow soup bowls and top with the prawns and sausage Creole.

Cool Hand Luke's Brunch Burrito

Paul Newman's movie provided the inspiration for Timothy Conrad's recipe, which naturally contains scrambled eggs. Timothy said, 'Cool Hand Luke's hard-boiled bet may have been easier to swallow if he had followed my recipe.' Timothy gave his award from this 1991 contest winner to the Columbus Children's Hospital.

SERVES 4

2 tablespoons vegetable oil
250g (8oz) sausagemeat
2 jalapeño chillies, seeded and chopped
1 onion, chopped
475ml (16fl oz) Newman's Own All-Natural Diavolo Sauce, or your favourite
8 eggs

salt and freshly ground black pepper
15g (½oz) unsalted butter
4 large flour tortillas, warmed
125g (4oz) Monterey Jack or Cheddar cheese, grated
shredded lettuce to garnish
1 lime, sliced

In a large nonstick frying pan, heat 1 tablespoon of the oil over medium heat. Add the sausage and cook thoroughly, breaking it up with a wooden spoon, until no pink shows. Remove from the pan and drain on kitchen paper. Wipe the fat from the pan.

In the same frying pan, heat the remaining oil over medium heat. Add the jalapeños and onion and cook, stirring, until tender. Add the sauce and sausage and cook for 5 minutes.

In a bowl, beat the eggs with 4 tablespoons of water, salt and pepper. In another frying pan, melt the butter over medium heat, pour in the eggs and cook, stirring, for 4 minutes. Stir in half of the sausage and sauce mixture.

Preheat the grill.

Spoon ¼ of the egg mixture onto each tortilla, then roll up the tortillas and place in an ovenproof or microwave-safe serving dish. Pour the remaining sausage and sauce over the tortillas and sprinkle the cheese on top. Grill or microwave the tortillas until the cheese melts.

Serve on plates garnished with the lettuce and lime slices.

The Woodward Veggyburger

What do you do when your husband is a hamburger devotee and you are inclined toward vegetarianism? Well, if you're Joanne Woodward, you invent the Veggyburger, which looks like a Newmanburger but contains no meat and can nestle in a bun just as appealingly as one of my minced beef specials. ■ SERVES 6 TO 8

125g (4oz) onion, chopped

2 tablespoons finely chopped garlic

1 tablespoon vegetable oil

3 tablespoons chopped fresh basil or 2 teaspoons dried

375g (12oz) cooked brown rice

25g (1oz) cashews

25g (1oz) walnuts

25g (1oz) almonds

25g (1oz) sunflower seeds

4 tablespoons tamari sauce (concentrated soy sauce)

150ml (¼ pint) tahini (sesame seed paste)

In a frying pan, sauté the onions and garlic in the oil. When the onions are translucent, add the basil and mix well. Add the mixture to the cooked rice.

Lightly toast the nuts in a frying pan and allow to cool. In a blender or food processor, grind all the nuts and sunflower seeds until coarsely ground. Add to the rice mixture with the tamari sauce and tahini. Shape into patties. To cook, brown in a nonstick pan.

Veggyburgers should be served in pitta bread or burger buns with your favourite accompaniments.

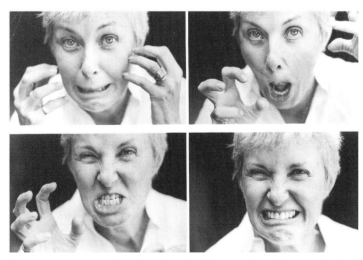

Joanne's reaction when she doesn't find a bottle of Newman's Own dressing in her cupboard

Twice-Baked Potato over Spinach, Broccoli and Peppers

These are not the typical stratospherically high-calorie stuffed potatoes. Different and definitely worth a try, and a whole potato makes a filling main course for any hungry vegetarian. The soy milk, soy bacon and soy cheese can all be found at any good health food store and at some better-stocked supermarkets. ■ SERVES 6

3 large potatoes, baked until soft
175ml (6fl oz) low-fat sour cream
4 tablespoons soy milk
40g (1½oz) unsalted butter
5 strips soy bacon, chopped
3 tablespoons chopped chives
salt and freshly ground black pepper to taste
250g (8oz) soy cheese (your favourite flavour), grated

VEGETABLES

4 tablespoons olive oil
1 tablespoon chopped garlic
1 large red pepper, seeded and cut into julienne strips
500g (1lb) broccoli florets
one 300g (10oz) pack frozen chopped spinach, defrosted and squeezed of liquid
4 tablespoons dry white wine
salt and freshly ground black pepper to taste
125ml (4fl oz) Newman's Own Bombolina Spaghetti Sauce, or your favourite
50g (2oz) grated soy Parmesan cheese for garnish
chopped basil for garnish

Preheat the oven to 230°C, 450°F, gas mark 8.

Leave the potatoes until cool enough to handle, then cut in half and scoop out the insides. Reserve the shells.

In a saucepan, combine the potatoes with the sour cream, milk and butter, and mash over low heat until combined. Add the bacon, chives, salt and pepper, and stir to combine. Spoon the filling into the shells, rounding the tops nicely, and sprinkle with the cheese.

Place the stuffed halves in a roasting tin and cover loosely with foil. Bake, covered, for 15 minutes. Remove the foil and bake for 5 minutes more.

While the potatoes are baking, prepare the vegetables. In a large saucepan, heat the oil over high heat until hot. Add the garlic and pepper and cook, stirring, for 5 minutes. Add the broccoli and cook, tossing, for 4 minutes. Add the spinach, wine, salt and pepper. Stir in the sauce, cover, lower the heat to medium and simmer for 7 minutes.

To serve, divide the vegetables among 6 plates. Place a stuffed potato half on top and sprinkle with some of the Parmesan cheese and basil.

Nell Newman's Marinated Ginger Tofu over Crispy Browned Soba Noodles

I used to buy tofu occasionally and attempted to scramble it or eat it raw, only to be disgusted by its lack of flavour. I finally discovered that tofu is mainly a carrier for flavours. It is very rich in protein and contains no cholesterol. If you are willing to experiment, you can make anything from main courses to desserts with it.

For this dinner recipe you can use just about any vegetable you want, particularly Chinese vegetables, which require less cooking time than many Western ones. Delicate vegetables such as bok choy (which can be found in Asian markets and many supermarkets) and red peppers should not be simmered with the tofu but placed in the marinade before putting the dish in the oven.

Even if you have never tried tofu and are generally sceptical about new foods, I promise you will enjoy this dish! ▓ **SERVES 4**

500g (1lb) tofu, cubed
150ml (¼ pint) tamari sauce or soy sauce
2 teaspoons peeled, grated root ginger
1 large onion, coarsely chopped
½ large red pepper, seeded and chopped

2 stalks celery, sliced 5mm (¼in) thick
3 stalks bok choy
1 large courgette, sliced 1cm (½in) thick
250g (8oz) soba noodles
3 tablespoons sesame oil

Place the tofu, tamari sauce, ginger and onion in a saucepan with 500ml (17fl oz) of water. Simmer for 1 hour, then leave to marinate for at least 1 hour or up to 5 hours.

Preheat the oven to 180°C, 350°F, gas mark 4.

Place the red pepper, celery, bok choy and courgette in a large, shallow, ovenproof dish and pour the tofu and marinade over them. Braise for 30–60 minutes, depending on how you like your tofu or how much time you have. I usually cook it until the tofu is browned and the sauce is bubbly.

While the tofu is cooking, place the soba noodles in boiling water with 1 tablespoon of sesame oil and cook until al dente. Drain and place in a nonstick pan over medium-high heat. Add the remaining 2 tablespoons of sesame oil and spread the noodles so they cover the pan evenly. Cook until darkly browned or lightly burned. To serve, spoon the tofu mixture over individual portions of the fried noodles.

Potato and Cheese Quesadillas with Green and Red Sauces

A hashed brown potato filling makes these vegetarian quesadillas a little different and mighty good. If you cook the hashed browns and combine the green sauce ahead of time, all that's left to do is assemble the tortillas and fry them—not too taxing, all in all.

SERVES 4

8 corn tortillas
375g (12oz) Monterey Jack or Cheddar cheese, sliced
1 tablespoon vegetable oil for frying

HASHED BROWN POTATOES

1 tablespoon vegetable oil
175g (6oz) finely diced peeled potato
50g (2oz) red onion, chopped
4 tablespoons diced red pepper
1 spring onion, chopped
salt and freshly ground black pepper to taste

GREEN SAUCE

4 tomatillos, husked and chopped
¼ small onion, chopped
3 garlic cloves, chopped
½ small serrano or jalapeño chilli, seeded
4 tablespoons chopped coriander
1 tablespoon fresh lime juice
salt and freshly ground black pepper to taste

ACCOMPANIMENTS

one 325g (11oz) jar Newman's Own All-Natural Bandito Salsa, or your favourite
1 avocado, peeled, stoned and chopped
125ml (4fl oz) sour cream
chopped coriander

To make the hashed brown potatoes, heat the oil in a frying pan until hot. Add the potatoes and cook, tossing, for 5 minutes. Add the onion, pepper, spring onion, salt and pepper. Cook, turning occasionally, for about 10 minutes, until the potatoes are crispy and browned.

To make the green sauce, combine the tomatillos, onion, garlic, chilli, coriander, lime juice, salt and pepper in a blender with 4 tablespoons of water until smooth. Pour into a serving bowl.

To make the quesadillas, place ¼ of the hashed potatoes on 4 tortillas and top each with 75g (3oz) of the sliced cheese. Heat the vegetable oil in a large frying pan until hot. Add

2 filled tortillas, top each with a tortilla, and cook until lightly browned on the bottom. Turn and cook until the cheese is melted and the bottom is browned. Remove, keep warm, and cook the remaining tortillas in the same way.

Serve immediately with the green sauce and a bowl of salsa on the side. Have bowls of the avocado, sour cream and coriander alongside for serving.

Piñata Pockets

Joan Klearman of St Louis, Missouri, created a delicious, healthful Mexican dish that is impressive and yet easy to prepare; it was a 1993 finalist. Her festive tortilla 'piñatas', baked under a zesty topping of Newman's Own All-Natural Bandito Salsa, burst with a colourful surprise of vegetables and spices. Joan donated her prize money to the English Language School in St Louis. ■ SERVES 5

2 teaspoons vegetable oil

2 red peppers, seeded and chopped

1 large onion, chopped

1 tablespoon chilli powder

1 teaspoon ground cumin

2 plum tomatoes, chopped

one 475–575g (15–19oz) can black beans, rinsed and drained

one 300g (10oz) pack frozen sweetcorn

one 125g (4oz) can chopped mild green chillies, drained

one 125g (4oz) can (drained weight) stoned ripe olives, chopped

juice of 1 lime

10 flour or corn tortillas, 15cm (6in) in diameter

two 325g (11oz) jars Newman's Own All-Natural Bandito Salsa (mild, medium, or hot), or your favourite

125g (4oz) low-fat Monterey Jack or Cheddar cheese, grated

chopped parsley for garnish

light sour cream and sliced avocado for serving (optional)

Heat the oil over medium-high heat in a large saucepan. Add the peppers and onion, and cook until tender but still crisp. Add the chilli powder and cumin and cook for 1 minute. Stir in the tomatoes, black beans, corn, chillies, olives and lime juice, and bring to the boil. Lower the heat, cover and cook for 15 minutes to blend the flavours.

Preheat the oven to 180°C, 350°F, gas mark 4.

Spoon about 125ml (4fl oz) of the vegetable mixture down the centre of each tortilla, then roll up the tortilla to enclose the filling. Place the tortillas, seam side down, in a 32 x 23cm (13 x 9in) glass baking dish. Spoon the salsa over the tortillas and sprinkle on the cheese. Bake for 20 minutes, or until the salsa is hot and the cheese is melted.

To serve, garnish the piñatas with chopped parsley and serve with sour cream and sliced avocado as accompaniments.

Pastas, Pizza and Rice

Baked Macaroni with Lamb and Cheese

Rigatoni with Chicken Sausage and Artichokes

Cappellini with Sautéed Prawn Caesar ▪ The Hudsucker Pasta ▪ Tom Cruise's Linguine with Zesty Red Clam Sauce ▪ Shells with Red Sauce and Blue Cheese ▪ Nicole Kidman's Crispy Orechiette with Broccoli, Pine Nuts and Garlic ▪ Fettuccine Alfredo à la Newman ▪ David Copperfield's Spicy Penne with Fontina Cheese ▪ Venezia Sauce al Mare y Newmano ▪ Gene Shalit's Spaghetti Carbonara

Rigatoni with Fat-Free Rosemary-Spinach Pesto

Lasagna Primavera ▪ Italian Artichoke Pasta

Newman's Whitecap Pizza ▪ **Sundance Summer**

Risotto ▪ **Susan Sarandon's Risotto with Scallops**

and Asparagus

Baked Macaroni with Lamb and Cheese

Chances are you won't find minced lamb in the meat department of most supermarkets, which means you will have to ask the butcher to mince lamb for you; or you can use shoulder of lamb, diced, as a substitute. Like the best of made-from-scratch macaroni and cheese, this one soothes the soul. It is rich and comforting, and different. ■ SERVES 6

500g (1lb) small macaroni
1 tablespoon vegetable oil
4 garlic cloves, chopped
500g (1lb) minced lamb
one 300g (10oz) pack frozen chopped spinach, defrosted but not drained
250ml (8fl oz) double cream

one 250ml (8fl oz) can evaporated milk
250g (8oz) sharp Cheddar cheese, grated
50g (2oz) mozzarella cheese, shredded
125g (4oz) goat's cheese, crumbled
salt and freshly ground black pepper to taste

Preheat the oven to 230°C, 450°F, gas mark 8.

Bring a large pan of salted water to the boil. Add the macaroni and cook until tender but still firm.

Meanwhile, heat the oil in a large saucepan over high heat until hot. Add the garlic, lamb and spinach and cook, stirring, for 5 minutes, until the lamb is no longer pink. Add the cream and evaporated milk, and bring to the boil. Lower the heat to medium-high and cook the mixture for about 5 minutes until it almost coats the back of a spoon. Turn the heat to low and add 175g (6oz) of the Cheddar and all the mozzarella and goat's cheese, stirring until melted. Taste and season lightly with salt (the cheeses are quite salty) and more liberally with pepper.

Drain the macaroni well in a large colander, then place in a medium casserole. Add the cream sauce and toss to combine. Sprinkle the remaining Cheddar cheese on top and bake for 7–10 minutes, until bubbling.

Rigatoni with Chicken Sausage and Artichokes

If you roast the peppers and make the pesto for this in advance, you have a great dish that comes together easily, at the last minute if need be. It's entirely your call on which type of sausage to use—fresh or smoked both work. Serve with a simple green salad, good bread and a young red wine.

■ MAKES 300ML (½ PINT) OF PESTO ■ SERVES 6

PESTO

50g (2oz) chopped fresh basil
25g (1oz) pine nuts
2 garlic cloves, coarsely chopped
50g (2oz) freshly grated Parmesan cheese
125ml (4fl oz) olive oil
salt and freshly ground black pepper to taste

PASTA

500g (1lb) rigatoni
1 tablespoon olive oil
3 fresh or smoked chicken sausages, sliced 5mm (¼in) thick

4 roasted red peppers (page 137), cored, seeded and cut into julienne strips
one 175g (6oz) jar marinated artichoke hearts, drained and coarsely chopped
salt and freshly ground black pepper to taste
125ml (4fl oz) dry white wine
175ml (6fl oz) Newman's Own 'Say Cheese' Pasta Sauce, or your favourite
125g (4oz) Parmesan cheese, freshly grated

To make the pesto, combine the basil, pine nuts, garlic and cheese in a blender or food processor and blend until coarsely chopped. With the machine running, add the oil slowly, blending until combined. Season with salt and pepper. Set aside.

Bring a large pot of salted water to the boil, add the rigatoni, and cook until firm but tender.

Meanwhile, heat the oil in a large frying pan until hot. Add the fresh sausage and cook, turning the pieces until browned on all sides. If using smoked sausage, toss the pieces in the oil just to coat. Add the pepper strips, artichoke hearts, salt and pepper and cook, stirring, until heated through. Add the wine and cook for 30–40 seconds. Add the sauce and cook, stirring until heated through, 1–2 minutes. Remove the pan from the heat.

To Roast Red Bell Peppers

There are several ways to roast fresh peppers: on the barbecue, directly over the flame on a gas stove, or in a lightly oiled cast-iron frying pan. The goal is to cook them until blackened on all sides. No matter how you choose to do it, use tongs to turn them.

When the peppers are charred—really black all over—remove them from the heat andallow to cool until you can handle them. Then put the peppers under running water and peel off the black. Some little bits and pieces may not want to come off, and that is fine. Core the peppers and seed them. They can be used in salads, as part of an antipasto, or in a recipe such as Rigatoni with Chicken Sausage and Artichokes (page 136).

You can also buy roasted peppers in jars in the supermarket. The ones you roast yourself, though, have a freshness and sweetness of flavour that can't be matched.

Drain the pasta. Still off the heat, add the pasta to the hot sauce with 50g (2oz) of the cheese and half of the pesto. Toss well and adjust the seasonings to taste. Refrigerate or freeze the remaining pesto for another use.

Serve immediately in heated bowls, with the remaining cheese on the side.

Cappellini with Sautéed Prawn Caesar

Here is another simple, mighty fine dish that needs nothing more than a green salad and a loaf of good bread. We like it with Chianti, although a bottle of white wine would be okay, too. ■ SERVES 6

2 tablespoons olive oil

3 garlic cloves, slivered

30 raw prawns, peeled and deveined

1 large red onion, cut into julienne
    strips

1 large red pepper, seeded and cut into
    julienne strips

175g (6oz) fresh, or frozen and
    defrosted, peas

500g (1lb) cappellini

175ml (6fl oz) Newman's Own Caesar
    Dressing, or your favourite

75g (3oz) freshly grated Parmesan
    cheese

salt and freshly ground black pepper to
    taste

Bring a large pan of salted water to the boil.

Meanwhile, heat the oil in a large frying pan or sauté pan over medium-high heat until hot. Add the garlic and cook until golden. Add the prawns and cook, tossing, until barely pink. With a slotted spoon transfer the prawns to a plate and cover loosely. Add the onion, pepper and peas to the pan and cook, stirring, until the onion is softened and the pepper is tender but still crisp, about 5 minutes. Return the prawns to the pan and sauté briefly, stirring to combine with the vegetables and warm through. Be careful not to overcook. Remove from the heat and keep warm.

Add the pasta to the boiling water, stirring to separate the strands, and cook until tender but al dente. Drain and place in a large heated bowl. Add the prawn sauce, dressing and 50g (2oz) of the Parmesan. Toss well and season with salt and pepper.

Serve immediately in heated bowls, with the remaining Parmesan on the side.

The Hudsucker Pasta

Shannon Wiggs, an assistant school principal, loves creamy, tomato-based pasta sauces. She discovered that prawns cooked together with Newman's Own Bombolina Spaghetti Sauce, Neufchâtel cheese, fresh mushrooms and sun-dried tomatoes, served over pasta, made for a quick, flavourful and elegant dish. A 1995 runner-up, she donated her award to Nativity House in Tacoma, Washington. ■ SERVES 4

3 garlic cloves, crushed

2 tablespoons olive oil

250g (8oz) mushrooms, sliced

125g (4oz) sun-dried tomatoes packed in oil, drained and chopped

475ml (16fl oz) Newman's Own Bombolina Spaghetti Sauce, or your favourite

4 tablespoons dry red wine

1 tablespoon balsamic vinegar

¼ teaspoon crushed red pepper flakes

125g (4oz) Neufchâtel or cream cheese, cubed

625g (1¼lb) raw prawns, peeled and deveined

375g (12oz) penne

50g (2oz) Parmesan cheese, grated

25g (1oz) pine nuts, toasted

chopped parsley for serving

In a 30cm (12in) frying pan, sauté the garlic in the olive oil over medium heat for 2 minutes. Add the mushrooms and sauté until tender. Add the tomatoes, sauce, wine, vinegar and crushed red pepper flakes and simmer for 7 minutes. Add the Neufchâtel cheese and stir until it melts. Add the prawns and simmer until they turn opaque throughout, about 5 minutes.

Meanwhile, cook the penne in boiling salted water until al dente. Drain and place in a large serving bowl.

Top the pasta with the prawn sauce. Sprinkle with the Parmesan, pine nuts and parsley, toss, and serve immediately.

Tom Cruise's Linguine with Zesty Red Clam Sauce

This is not your typical red clam sauce. You use freshly steamed clams here, served in their shells, in a light tomato sauce, heady with garlic, that is peppery too.

To crush garlic, use the same technique you do to peel it. First separate the cloves from the head. Put the flat side of a knife down on one garlic clove at a time and with your other hand smack the knife right over the clove. This should split the garlic peel with one whack. If it doesn't, try again. Remove the skins and use the cloves whole. ■ **MAKES ABOUT 1 LITRE (1¾ PINTS) OF SAUCE** ■ **SERVES 6**

TOMATO SAUCE

125ml (4fl oz) olive oil

8 garlic cloves, crushed

4 tablespoons capers, undrained

60g (2½oz) chopped parsley, plus extra for garnish

500g (1lb) chopped plum tomatoes

175ml (6fl oz) fresh lemon juice

175ml (6fl oz) dry white wine

½ teaspoon crushed red pepper flakes

1 teaspoon salt

1 heaped teaspoon freshly ground black pepper

PASTA

500g (1lb) linguine

CLAMS

30 clams, scrubbed

8 garlic cloves, chopped

250ml (8fl oz) dry white wine

250ml (8fl oz) vegetable stock or water

To make the tomato sauce, heat the oil in a large saucepan until hot. Add the garlic and capers, then carefully add the parsley. Stand back because the oil may spatter. Add the tomatoes, lemon juice, wine, pepper flakes, salt and black pepper. Cook, stirring occasionally, for 15 minutes.

Bring a large pan of salted water to the boil. Add the linguine and cook until firm but tender.

While the pasta is cooking, steam the clams. Place the clams in another large pan with the garlic, wine and vegetable stock. Cover and bring to the boil over high heat, shaking the pan until all the shells are open. Leaving the open clams in the pan, drain off all but 4 tablespoons of the liquid and stir it into the tomato sauce. Cover the clams and keep warm while preparing the rest of the dish.

Drain the linguine and add to the tomato sauce. Cook over high heat for about 4 minutes to heat through.

Divide the pasta among 6 heated bowls. Top each serving with 5 clams and garnish with the remainng parsley.

Shells with Red Sauce and Blue Cheese This is
simple, tasty, and quick. It is ready in the time it takes to cook the shells.

SERVES 6

500g (1lb) small pasta shells

2 tablespoons olive oil

4 garlic cloves, chopped

250g (8oz) fresh tomatoes, chopped

one 300g (10oz) pack frozen peas, defrosted

salt and freshly ground black pepper to taste

125g (4oz) good-quality blue cheese, crumbled

125ml (4fl oz) Newman's Own Industrial Strength Venetian Spaghetti Sauce with Mushrooms, or your favourite

2 tablespoons freshly grated Parmesan cheese for serving

Bring a large pot of salted water to the boil, add the pasta, and cook until tender but al dente. Drain well and keep warm.

Meanwhile, make the sauce. Heat the oil in a medium sauté pan over high heat until hot. Add the garlic, tomatoes, peas, salt and pepper and cook, stirring occasionally, for 5 minutes. Add the drained pasta and toss until combined. Stir in the blue cheese and sauce and toss until mixed.

Divide the pasta among 6 pasta bowls or plates and sprinkle each serving with a little Parmesan cheese.

Nicole Kidman's Crispy Orechiette with Broccoli, Pine Nuts and Garlic
This is a one-of-a-kind dish. The great appeal is the orechiette: it is meant to be crunchy. Don't jump the gun when you are cooking the pasta and take it out before it is crisp.

■ SERVES 6

1kg (2lb) orechiette (little ears)
175ml (6fl oz) vegetable oil
2 tablespoons slivered garlic
500g (1lb) small broccoli florets
75ml (3fl oz) dry white wine
4 tablespoons fresh lemon juice
salt and freshly ground black pepper to
    taste

3 tablespoons balsamic vinegar
75g (3oz) unsalted butter, cut in chunks
    and softened
50g (2oz) pine nuts, toasted
125g (4oz) Parmesan cheese, freshly
    grated

In a large pan, cook the orechiette in plenty of salted boiling water until tender but firm. Drain, run under cold water, and drain well again.

Have ready 2 medium sauté pans. Heat 4 tablespoons of oil in each until smoking. Add the cooked orechiette carefully to the hot oil, dividing it equally. Spread the pasta out in even layers and cook for about 3 minutes, or until medium brown on the underside. Turn the pasta over and cook without stirring until browned on the other side. Transfer the pasta and oil to a large bowl and keep warm.

Heat the remaining oil in one pan until hot. Add the garlic and broccoli and sauté, tossing, for 5 minutes. Add the wine, lemon juice, salt and pepper. Taste, adjust the seasonings if necessary, and cook for 3 minutes. Transfer to a large flameproof baking dish.

Add the browned orechiette, balsamic vinegar, butter and pine nuts to the baking dish and toss over medium-high heat until the butter is melted. Add half the cheese and toss to combine.

Serve the pasta in 6 heated bowls or plates, with a generous grinding of fresh black pepper on top and the remaining cheese on the side.

Fettuccine Alfredo à la Newman
Fettuccine Alfredo has never been credited with any dietary virtues, only gustatory ones—and lots of them. This rendition is slightly different: It has less butter but more cream than usual, an egg yolk (which makes up for the missing butter), and peas. If we hadn't pointed it out to you, you probably wouldn't even have known the butter wasn't there. Don't let the cream put you off. This is very good, and tomorrow is another day, as someone once said. ■ SERVES 6

500g (1lb) fettuccine
1 teaspoon unsalted butter
250g (8oz) frozen baby peas, defrosted
4 tablespoons dry white wine
juice of 1 lemon
350ml (12fl oz) double cream
1 egg yolk

150g (5oz) Parmesan cheese, freshly grated
1 teaspoon salt
1 tablespoon freshly ground black pepper
chopped Italian flat-leaf parsley for garnish (optional)

Bring a large pan of salted water to the boil. Add the fettuccine and cook until firm but tender.

Meanwhile, melt the butter in a large saucepan over medium-high heat. Add the peas and cook for 1 minute. Add the white wine and lemon juice and reduce the mixture by half. Add the cream and cook over high heat for 4–5 minutes, until it almost coats a spoon. Remove the pan from the heat and quickly whisk in the egg yolk. Add 125g (4oz) of the cheese, salt and pepper, and whisk rapidly to combine well.

Drain the fettuccine, add it to the saucepan, and toss quickly, until coated.

Serve the fettuccine immediately, garnished with the parsley and with the remaining Parmesan on the side.

David Copperfield's Spicy Penne with Fontina Cheese

If you grow your own basil, you are in luck here; you'll need a *big* bunch for this recipe. The remaining ingredients are straight-forward and simple, and together they add up to a satisfying sauce. The key is in letting the fontina only partially melt. ■ SERVES 6

500g (1lb) penne
4 tablespoons olive oil
250g (8oz) frozen peas, defrosted
2 small onions, cut into julienne strips
25g (1oz) chopped basil leaves
4 tablespoons dry white wine
juice of 1 lemon

350ml (12fl oz) Newman's Own All-Natural Diavolo Sauce, or your favourite
½ teaspoon crushed red pepper flakes
250g (8oz) fontina cheese, grated
salt (optional)
fresh Parmesan cheese for grating at the table

Bring a large pan of salted water to the boil. Add the penne and cook until tender but firm. Drain well and keep warm.

Meanwhile, heat the oil in a large sauté pan over high heat until hot. Add the peas, onions and basil leaves and cook, stirring, for 5 minutes. Add the wine and lemon juice, and cook for 3 minutes. Add the sauce and pepper flakes and bring to a simmer, stirring, until hot. Stir in the fontina cheese and cook for barely 30 seconds, until semi-melted.

Add the penne to the sauce and toss well. Taste and add salt if needed.

Serve at once in heated bowls, sprinkled with the Parmesan.

Venezia Sauce al Mare y Newmano

Newman's Own Industrial Strength Venetian Spaghetti Sauce with Mushrooms is quickly and elegantly transformed by the flavourful addition of green olives, capers, sultanas and pine nuts in Cheryll McDowell's 1995 finalist recipe. She initially developed this to be used over prawns but has found that chicken is an outstanding substitute. Cheryll donated her award to Susan G. Koman Breast Cancer Research Foundation and Friends of the Cowlitz. ■ SERVES 6

500g (1lb) vermicelli
½ teaspoon crushed red pepper flakes
1 teaspoon extra virgin olive oil
one 800g (26oz) jar Newman's Own
    Industrial Strength Venetian
    Spaghetti Sauce with Mushrooms,
    or your favourite
75g (3oz) green olives

4 tablespoons capers
40g (1½oz) sultanas
25g (1oz) pine nuts
1 tablespoon chopped fresh basil
1 tablespoon chopped fresh parsley
625g (1¼lb) large raw prawns, peeled
    and deveined

Cook the vermicelli in a large pan of boiling, salted water until tender but firm.

Meanwhile, in a 30cm (12in) frying pan, cook the crushed red pepper flakes in the oil for 2 minutes. Add the sauce and green olives and cook until the sauce begins to bubble, about 5 minutes.

Add the capers, sultanas, pine nuts, basil and parsley and cook for 5 minutes.

Add the prawns and bring the mixture to the boil. Lower the heat to medium, cover the pan and cook for 5 minutes, or until the prawns turn opaque throughout. Stir 125ml (4fl oz) of the pasta cooking water into the sauce.

Drain the vermicelli. Serve the pasta with the prawn sauce on top.

Gene Shalit's Spaghetti Carbonara

There is a surprise ingredient in this version of spaghetti carbonara—fresh tomatoes. They add colour and tang to what is an unspeakably indulgent dish that you have to have every now and then as a reminder of just how delicious it is. ■ SERVES 6

500g (1lb) spaghetti
1 tablespoon olive oil
1 tablespoon chopped garlic
50g (2oz) diced onion
500g (1lb) plum tomatoes, chopped
350ml (12fl oz) double cream
8 strips bacon, cooked, drained and
    crumbled

½ teaspoon salt
½ teaspoon freshly ground black
    pepper
75g (3oz) freshly grated Parmesan
    cheese
Italian flat-leaf parsley, finely chopped,
    for garnish

Bring a large pan of salted water to the boil. Add the spaghetti and cook until firm but tender.

Meanwhile, heat the oil in a large sauté pan over high heat until hot. Add the garlic, onion and tomatoes and cook, stirring, for 8 minutes. Add the cream and cook for about 5 minutes to reduce it by about one quarter. Stir in the bacon, salt and pepper until combined. Remove the pan from the heat.

Drain the pasta, add it at once to the sauce, and toss to coat. Put the pan over medium heat and add 25g (1oz) of the cheese. Toss until the cheese is fully blended in and the strands are well coated.

Serve at once, garnished with the parsley and with the remaining cheese on the side.

Rigatoni with Fat-Free Rosemary-Spinach Pesto

Classic Italian pesto is made with fresh basil plus oil, cheese and nuts—quite a payload when it comes to fat. Even if the pesto we have here isn't authentic, it is a terrific sauce, especially with pasta. It is also wonderful as a spread or dip. You'll have some left over, so you can see how you like it best.

■ **MAKES ABOUT 350ML (12FL OZ) OF PESTO** ■ **SERVES 6**

500g (1lb) rigatoni

4 tablespoons olive oil

2 tablespoons slivered garlic

3–4 asparagus stalks, depending on size, halved

150g (5oz) yellow squash, peeled and cut into 5mm(¼in)

¼ teaspoon salt

½ teaspoon freshly ground black pepper

350ml (12fl oz) Newman's Own 'Say Cheese' Pasta Sauce, or your favourite

50g (2oz) Parmesan cheese, freshly grated (optional)

ROSEMARY-SPINACH PESTO

50g (2oz) spinach leaves, chopped, rinsed and patted dry fresh

2 tablespoons fresh rosemary

2 tablespoons chopped garlic

2 tablespoons chopped onion

4 tablespoons rice wine vinegar

juice of 1 orange

salt and freshly ground black pepper to taste

To make the pesto, combine the spinach, rosemary, garlic, onion, vinegar, orange juice, salt and pepper in a blender and blend until puréed. (Adjust the consistency by adding more orange juice to thin the pesto if desired.) If made in advance, store the pesto in the refrigerator, covered with a piece of clingfilm directly on the surface to prevent the sauce from discolouring; it will keep for 1 week.

Bring a large pan of salted water to the boil. Add the rigatoni and cook until tender but firm.

Meanwhile, heat the oil in a frying pan until hot. Add the garlic, asparagus, squash, salt and pepper and sauté, stirring, for 3 minutes. Stir in the sauce and cook over medium heat, stirring, until hot and the pasta is cooked.

Drain the rigatoni and place in a large bowl. Add the vegetable sauce and toss. Add 175ml (6fl oz) of the pesto and toss again.

Serve at once in wide, heated pasta bowls, sprinkled with the Parmesan.

Lasagna Primavera

Lasagna Primavera This is a light and beautiful lasagna. Janet Sutherland's clever method of blanching the fresh vegetables with the pasta streamlines the preparation. Janet won the 1992 grand prize for this recipe and donated the money to the Assistance League of Escondido Valley. ▨ SERVES 8

250g (8oz) lasagna
3 carrots, cut into 5mm (¼in) slices
75g (3oz) broccoli florets
125g (4oz) courgette, cut into 5mm (¼in) slices
1 summer squash, cut into 5mm (¼in) slices
two 300g (10oz) pack frozen chopped spinach, defrosted

250g (8oz) ricotta cheese
one 800g (26oz) jar Newman's Own All-Natural Marinara Style Spaghetti Sauce with Mushrooms, or your favourite
375g (12oz) mozzarella cheese, thinly sliced
50g (2oz) Parmesan cheese, grated

Preheat the oven to 200°C, 400°F, gas mark 6. Line a 37 x 25cm (15 x 10in) baking sheet with foil.

Bring 4 litres (6½ pints) of water to the boil in a large saucepan over high heat. Add the lasagna and cook for 5 minutes. Add the carrots and cook 2 minutes more. Add the broccoli, courgette and squash and cook for 2 minutes more, or until the pasta is tender. Drain the lasagne and vegetables well.

Squeeze any liquid from the spinach. Combine the spinach with the ricotta.

Spread ⅓ of the sauce on the bottom of a large rectangular baking tin. Line the tin with half the lasagna. Top with half of each vegetable, half the spinach mixture, and half the mozzarella. Pour half of the remaining sauce over the top. Continue to make layers with the remaining ingredients, ending with a layer of sauce. Sprinkle the Parmesan over the sauce.

Bake the lasagna, uncovered, on the prepared baking sheet for approximately 30 minutes, or until hot in the centre. Leave to stand for 10 minutes before serving.

The lasagna may be prepared up to 2 days in advance and kept covered in the refrigerator. If chilled, bake the lasagna at 180°C, 350°F, gas mark 4 for 1 hour.

Serve with Italian bread or rolls, a green salad with Newman's Own Light Italian Dressing, and red wine.

Italian Artichoke Pasta

A group effort headed by the Sunset Hill P.T.A. fund-raising chairman challenged parents to create winning recipes. They succeeded with this 1996 runner-up. Newman's Own gives high marks to Sue Kakuk, John Cro, and the Sunset Hill PTA in Plymouth, Minnesota, for this recipe, which is easy to make and very impressive to serve. The award went to the Sunset Hill PTA. ■ SERVES 6 AS A MAIN DISH

4 teaspoons olive oil

1 large skinless, boneless chicken breast, cut into 5cm (2in) pieces

500g (1lb) linguine

250g (8oz) mushrooms, sliced

1 garlic clove, finely choppedone 250g (8oz) bottle Newman's Own Olive Oil and Vinegar Dressing, or your favourite

one 425g (14oz) can artichoke hearts, drained and cut into quarters

600ml (1 pint) cherry tomatoes, cut in half

freshly grated Parmesan cheese

Heat 2 teaspoons of the oil in a 25cm (10in) nonstick frying pan over medium-high heat. Add the chicken and cook for 3–5 minutes, turning, until tender and opaque. Remove the chicken from the pan and keep warm.

Meanwhile, cook the linguine in a large pan of boiling, salted water until tesnder but firm. Drain and keep warm.

In the frying pan, heat the remaining 2 teaspoons of oil, add the mushrooms, and cook until their juice evaporates and they are browned. Add the garlic and cook for 1–2 minutes. Stir in the dressing, artichoke hearts and cherry tomatoes. Cover and cook over medium heat for 5 minutes. Add the chicken and cook until heated through.

Divide the hot pasta among 6 plates or pasta bowls, top each serving with sauce, and sprinkle with the cheese.

Newman's Whitecap Pizza
Linda Mangen of Valrico, Florida, put a new twist on a classic pizza for her winning recipe. This 1992 finalist gave her award to the University of Tampa Scholarship Fund. ■ SERVES 4

500g (1lb) skinless, boneless chicken breast
one 500g (16oz) bottle Newman's Olive Oil and Vinegar Dressing or Newman's Own Light Italian Dressing, or your favourite
1 ready-to-bake pizza crust

250g (8oz) feta cheese, crumbled
one 125g (4oz) can artichoke hearts
250g (8oz) mozzarella cheese, shredded
4 lettuce leaves
2 beefsteak tomatoes, sliced
one 125g (4oz) can sliced black olives

Cut the chicken into bite-sized pieces and place in a glass bowl with half the salad dressing. Marinate in the refrigerator for 3–5 hours.

Preheat the oven to 200°C, 400°F, gas mark 6.

Brush a large baking sheet with 2 tablespoons of salad dressing. Lay the pizza crust on the baking sheet. Brush the top of the pizza crust with 2 tablespoons of dressing.

Drain the chicken. In a hot frying pan sauté the chicken for approximately 5 minutes, or until all the liquid has evaporated.

Sprinkle the feta over the pizza crust. Drain the artichoke hearts and squeeze out any excess moisture. Tear the artichokes into bite-size pieces. Place the chicken and artichoke hearts over the feta, covering the entire pizza. Sprinkle the mozzarella over all.

Bake the pizza for 15–18 minutes. Remove, leave to stand for 2 minutes, then cut into 8 wedges.

Serve the pizza with 4 individual bowls of salad. Combine the lettuce, sliced beefsteak tomatoes and sliced olives, then drizzle each salad with some of the remaining dressing.

Sundance Summer Risotto

This is a great-looking, great-tasting risotto, made with a slight twist: the stock isn't heated before it is added to the rice. Have 1.5 litres (2½ pints) of stock on hand, but you may not need all of it—you'll probably use 5 cups at most. What is the only way to know when a risotto is ready to serve, when the rice is creamy and firm but not hard? Taste it, and keep tasting it until it is right. But you should do that whenever you cook.

■ **SERVES 6**

RISOTTO

1 teaspoon olive oil
25g (1oz) red onion, finely chopped
425g (14oz) Arborio rice
250ml (8fl oz) dry white wine
1–1.5 litres (1¾–2½ pints) homemade or natural (MSG-free) chicken or vegetable stock

1 teaspoon olive oil
2 asparagus stalks, cut on the diagonal into 1cm (½in) pieces
125g (4oz) tomato, chopped
175g (6oz) fresh or frozen sweetcorn
salt and freshly ground black pepper
75g (3oz) Parmesan cheese, freshly grated

To make the risotto, heat the oil in a large saucepan over medium-high heat until hot. Add the onion and cook, stirring, until translucent. Add the rice and stir to coat it evenly. Stir in the wine and cook for 1–2 minutes. Add the stock by the ladleful, stirring it slowly into the rice until fully absorbed. Keep adding the stock by the ladleful and stirring it in. The risotto is done when the mixture is creamy but the rice is firm to the bite, a total of about 20–25 minutes. There should be almost no liquid remaining in the pan. Do not feel obliged to use all the stock, but do stir constantly.

While the risotto is cooking, heat the 1 teaspoon of oil in a frying pan until hot. Add the asparagus, tomato and corn and cook, stirring, until tender but still csrisp. Season with salt and pepper.

Stir the hot risotto into the vegetables and combine well. Stir in 50g (2oz) of the cheese until blended.

Serve at once in bowls, with the remaining cheese as garnish.

Susan Sarandon's Risotto with Scallops and Asparagus

This is a springtime risotto if there ever was one. If you can enlist a sous-chef or helper at the stove for the last few minutes of cooking, do so. One of you should stir the risotto; the other should attend to the scallops and vegetables. With attention like that to each part of the dish, there's much less likelihood of overcooking the scallops, something you don't want to do. ■ SERVES 6

RISOTTO

1 teaspoon olive oil
25g (1oz) red onion, finely chopped
425g (14oz) Arborio rice
250ml (8fl oz) dry white wine
1–1.5 litres (1¾–2½ pints) homemade or natural (MSG-free) chicken or vegetable stock

1 teaspoon olive oil
1 tablespoon finely chopped garlic
12 small scallops
250g (8oz) chopped tomatoes
2 asparagus stalks, cut into 1cm (½in) pieces on the diagonal
salt and freshly ground black pepper
75g (3oz) Parmesan cheese, freshly grated

Make the risotto following the directions on page 154.

While you are cooking the risotto, heat the oil in a large frying pan over medium-high heat until hot. Add the garlic and cook, stirring, until fragrant but not coloured. Add the scallops and toss quickly with the garlic. Add the tomatoes and asparagus, and sauté the mixture, tossing until the scallops are cooked through and the vegetables are tender but still crisp, about 5–10 minutes. Remove the pan from the heat and season with salt and pepper.

Add the risotto to the scallops and vegetables, and stir to combine well. Taste and adjust the seasonings. Stir in 50g (2oz) of the cheese.

Serve at once in heated bowls or soup plates, with the remaining cheese on the side.

Vegetables and Side Dishes

Sautéed Beetroot Greens

Newman's Creamed Spinach ▪ Grilled Vegetables ▪

Caramelized East Indian Vegetables ▪ Balsamic

Aubergine and Potatoes ▪ Garlicky Mashed Potatoes

▪ Honey Mustard Mashed Potatoes ▪ Roasted Herbed

New Potatoes with Spinach ▪ Potato Salad with Two

Mustards Dressing ▪ Creamy Potato Salad ▪ Braised

Root Vegetables ▪ Yam Gratin ▪ Sandy Austin's

Brown Rice Salad ▪ Butch's Wild West Tex-Mex Salad

The dishes I concoct—in my sleep, at the racetrack, and elsewhere—usually incorporate meat, but Joanne prefers meals that use vegetables, whole grains, and natural foods. So dinner at our house is as likely to feature brown rice or tofu as beef.

While the following recipes can be served as side dishes in smaller portions, many are hearty enough to serve as main courses. Just toss a salad, slice some homemade bread, and serve.

—PAUL NEWMAN

Cross-dressing for the 1996 camp gala

Sautéed Beetroot Greens

Substitute well-rinsed spinach or Swiss chard here if you are unable to find beetroot greens. The tofu contributes a nice creaminess and makes this more of a main dish for vegetarians. If tofu is not for you, leave it out. ■ **SERVES 6**

875g (1¾lb) beetroot greens

1 tablespoon olive oil

1 garlic clove, finely chopped

3 shallots, coarsely chopped

140g (4½oz) firm tofu, diced (optional)

4 tablespoons dry white wine

2 tablespoons toasted sesame seeds

15g (½oz) unsalted butter

¼ teaspoon Worcestershire sauce

Remove the stems of the beetroot greens, rinse the leaves well, and shred the leaves. Pat dry with kitchen paper.

Heat the oil in a large frying pan over medium heat until hot. Add the garlic and shallots, and cook, stirring, until the shallots are just softened. Raise the heat to medium-high and add the beetroot greens. Sauté, tossing, until the leaves wilt, 5–7 minutes.

Lower the heat to medium. Add the tofu, wine and sesame seeds, and toss gently until heated through. Stir in the butter and Worcestershire sauce.

Serve hot.

Newman's Creamed Spinach
Very simple, very rich, and very, very good. ■ SERVES 4

500g (1lb) fresh spinach	**75g (3oz) cream cheese, softened**
⅛ teaspoon ground nutmeg	**125ml (4fl oz) double cream**

Wash the spinach well and trim the stems. Place the spinach in a saucepan with just the water that clings to the leaves. Sprinkle with the nutmeg, cover, and steam for 2–3 minutes, until the leaves are wilted. Drain any excess liquid. Finely chop the spinach and return to the saucepan.

Beat the cream cheese in a small bowl until fluffy. Gradually beat in the double cream until blended. Stir the cream cheese mixture into the chopped spinach. Cook over medium heat, stirring frequently, until blended and creamy. Serve immediately.

Grilled Vegetables

Grilled vegetables are great with any barbecue or roast, or use them as an ingredient in green or rice salads, omelettes or even frittatas. We've made extra here, and once you have the barbecue going, why not? Vary the vegetables as you like. Another good choice is fresh fennel, cut into thick slices. ■ SERVES 12

125ml (4fl oz) olive oil, or more to taste
1 tablespoon Worcestershire sauce
1 tablespoon balsamic vinegar
spike seasoning to taste
4 tablespoons chopped fresh basil
6 corn cobs, shucked and cut in half
1 large aubergine, cut lengthwise into
    6 slices and halved
2 large courgettes, trimmed, cut into
    thirds, and halved

2 red peppers, cored, seeded and cut
    into quarters
2 green peppers, cored, seeded and cut
    into quarters
3 bunches spring onions, trimmed and
    halved
1 yam, peeled and thinly sliced
freshly ground black pepper to taste
Newman's Own Ranch Dressing and
    Newman's Own Caesar Dressing,
    or your favourite, for dipping

Light the barbecue and leave until hot.

In a roasting tin, combine the oil, Worcestershire sauce, vinegar, spike seasoning and basil. Add all the vegetables and toss to coat.

Grill the vegetables in a hinged grill basket about 10cm (4in) from the heat. Allow about 10 minutes, turning frequently, for the corn; 4 minutes per side for the courgettes; 3½ minutes per side for the peppers; 2½–3 minutes per side for the aubergine; 2–4 minutes per side for the yam slices; and 2–3 minutes, turning frequently, for the spring onions.

Serve the vegetables on a platter. Grind plenty of fresh pepper over them. Place the dressings in bowls for dipping.

NOTE: Spike seasoning is a mixture of assorted herbs and seaweed. It can be found in most health food stores.

Caramelized East Indian Vegetables These

vegetables can be used as an accompaniment to Danny Aiello's New York Sirloin Steak and His Cherokee Indian Curry AAA Steak Sauce (see page 65). Or try them as a bed on which to steam sea bass fillets in foil, or as a vegetarian sauce for pasta. They are four star as a topping for warm focaccia, too. ■ SERVES 6

6 carrots, peeled and cut into 2.5cm (1in) pieces

4 tablespoons vegetable oil

2 small Spanish onions, cut into julienne strips

1 small aubergine, about 375g (12oz), unpeeled but diced

4 tablespoons rice wine vinegar

50g (2oz) sugar

25g (1oz) unsalted butter

1 tablespoon ground cumin

1 teaspoon salt

1 teaspoon freshly ground black pepper

Parboil the carrots in a large saucepan of boiling water for about 10 minutes, until just soft when tested with a fork. Drain, run under cold water to stop the cooking, and pat dry with kitchen paper. Cover and refrigerate until ready to use.

Heat the oil in a large frying pan over medium-high heat until hot. Add the onions and aubergine and cook, tossing, for 8 minutes, until softened. Add the carrots and cook, tossing, for 5 minutes. Pour in the vinegar and cook for 2 minutes. Stir in the sugar until dissolved. The pan juices will thicken and look shiny. Add the butter, cumin, salt and pepper, and stir until the butter is melted and all the vegetables are coated.

Serve warm.

Balsamic Aubergine and Potatoes

For a really delightful mix of tastes and colours, pair this with Herbed Salmon Fillets in Foil (page 107). Serve the vegetables alongside or, better still, use them as a bed for the salmon. Any leftovers are great on hard rolls or crusty French bread.

SERVES 6

175ml (6fl oz) balsamic vinegar

4 tablespoons honey mustard

3 bunches spring onions, both green and white parts, trimmed and thinly sliced

half of a 250g (8oz) jar sun-dried tomatoes packed in oil, drained and cut into julienne strips

1.25kg (2½lb) potatoes, diced and reserved in cold water to cover

4 tablespoons vegetable oil

1 large aubergine, about 625g (1¼lb), unpeeled but diced

salt and freshly ground black pepper to taste

In a bowl, whisk the balsamic vinegar into the mustard. Stir in the spring onions and sun-dried tomatoes and set side.

Pat the potatoes dry with kitchen paper.

Heat 2 tablespoons of the oil in a large frying pan over high heat until hot. Add the potatoes and cook, tossing gently, for 8 minutes. In another frying pan, heat the remaining 2 tablespoons of oil over high heat until hot. Add the aubergine and cook, tossing occasionally, for 6 minutes. Add the aubergine to the potatoes. Pour in the balsamic vinegar mixture, toss to combine well, and cook over medium heat for about 2 minutes, until heated through. Season with lots of salt and pepper.

Serve hot or at room temperature.

Garlicky Mashed Potatoes

These mashed potatoes are fantastic when served with Garlic-Herb Marinated Halibut with Lemon Sauce (page 118) as well as with roasted meat or poultry or other types of fish. What they lack in butter is made up for by the double cream. If you're watching your fat intake, you can use milk instead. They'll still be tasty, but not as decadently satisfying.

Use an old-fashioned handheld masher. The hardware store variety that looks something like a short-handled hoe is the one to have. ■ SERVES 6

5 large baking potatoes
4 tablespoons chopped fresh basil
8 garlic cloves, chopped

475–500ml (16–18fl oz) double cream, or low-fat milk if you insist
salt and freshly ground black pepper to taste

Peel and quarter the potatoes, place in a large saucepan, and cover with cold water. Boil gently for 15–20 minutes, until soft when tested with a fork. Drain well and return to the saucepan.

Mash the potatoes with a potato masher, then stir in the basil and garlic. Add the cream slowly, stirring it in. Use enough to make the right consistency, creamy and fluffy. Season with salt and pepper.

Serve at once or spoon into a bowl, cover tightly with clingfilm, and set the bowl in a pan of hot water. Keep warm by setting the pan over a very low heat until ready to serve.

Honey Mustard Mashed Potatoes

These mashed potatoes were created to be served with Sarah Jessica Parker's Grilled Prawns with Vodka-Lime Sauce (page 119) for a super combination of sweet and sour flavours. They are also good with Lamb Chops in Minty Marinade (page 74) or Tony Randall's Grilled Veal Chop with Bourbon–Cracked Black Pepper Sauce (page 78). When you come right down to it, meat of almost any kind with mashed potatoes is a hard combo to improve on. For our convictions on potato mashers—a more important point than you might think when it comes to this singular dish—see the previous recipe on page 164. ▓ S E R V E S 6

5 large baking potatoes
475ml (16fl oz) double cream
3 tablespoons honey mustard
50g (2oz) unsalted butter, cut into
    chunks and softened

1½ tablespoons freshly ground black
    pepper
salt to taste

Peel, quarter, boil and drain the potatoes as directed in Garlicky Mashed Potatoes (page 164).

Return the potatoes to the saucepan and add half the cream, the mustard and butter. Mash with a potato masher, gradually adding more cream until you have the texture you like best. Add the pepper and fluff with a fork. Season with salt and serve at once, or kep warm in a bain-marie according to the directions on page 164.

Roasted Herbed New Potatoes with Spinach

These are mighty fine as is, but become unforgettable when served with Matthew Broderick's Grilled T-bone Steak with Sweet Onion Marmalade and Campfire Mustard Sauce (page 64). You'll need fresh tarragon, and if you can't find it, substitute another fresh herb (not dried) such as rosemary or basil. It's the combination of colours and fresh flavours that really sets these potatoes apart. ■ SERVES 6

12 small new red potatoes, scrubbed
4 tablespoons olive oil
1 tablespoon chopped fresh tarragon
salt and freshly ground black pepper to
    taste

300g (10oz) fresh spinach, washed,
    stems removed, patted dry and
    coarsely chopped

Preheat the oven to 230°C, 450°F, gas mark 8.

Place the potatoes in a large saucepan and cover with cold water. Boil gently over medium-high heat until soft, about 20 minutes. Drain, run under cold water to stop the cooking, and halve the potatoes.

Arrange in a single layer in a large glass baking dish. Add the oil, tarragon, salt and pepper. Toss gently to coat. Roast for 15 minutes.

Spread the spinach over the potatoes in an even layer and pour 125ml (4fl oz) of water into the dish. Roast for 5 minutes more.

Serve at once.

Potato Salad with Two Mustards Dressing

If you're looking for something socially acceptable or even well bred to serve with Whoopi Goldberg's Big Bad Ass Beef Ribs (page 68), this is it. It's also very good to take on picnics because, unlike a lot of potato salad we've had, this is mayo and oil free. ■ **SERVES 6**

6 medium red potatoes, scrubbed but not peeled

4 tablespoons seasoned rice wine vinegar

2 tablespoons honey mustard

1 tablespoon Dijon mustard

2 tablespoons capers, drained

2 stalks celery, finely chopped

salt and freshly ground black pepper to taste

Place the potatoes in a large saucepan and cover with cold water. Boil gently over medium-high heat for 15–20 minutes, until just tender when tested with a fork. Drain, run under cold water to stop the cooking, and cut into 8 pieces each.

In a large bowl, whisk together the vinegar and mustards. Stir in the capers. Add the potatoes and celery and toss. Season with salt and plenty of fresh pepper.

Creamy Potato Salad

The dressing on this potato salad is tangy and tart, and goes particularly well with Spice-Rubbed Roasted Turkey Breast (page 100) for a summer meal. If you don't have shallots, you can use sliced spring onion or finely chopped red onion instead. ■ SERVES 6

16 small new red potatoes, scrubbed
125ml (4fl oz) sour cream
4 tablespoons Dijon mustard
juice of 1 lemon

½ teaspoon salt
1 teaspoon freshly ground black pepper
4 shallots, finely chopped

Place the potatoes in a large saucepan and cover with cold water. Boil gently over medium heat for about 20 minutes, until just tender when tested with a fork. Drain, run under cold water to stop the cooking, and halve or quarter according to their size.

In a large salad bowl, whisk together the sour cream, mustard, lemon juice, salt and pepper. Add the potatoes and shallots and toss gently to combine. Serve immediately. If made ahead, cover and refrigerate. Remove and let it come to room temperature before serving.

Braised Root Vegetables

Three root vegetables—potatoes, parsnips and carrots—are featured in this braise that is terrific served alongside Tony Randall's Grilled Veal Chop with Bourbon–Cracked Black Pepper Sauce (page 78). A word of caution: don't confuse parsnips with turnips. Parsnips are carrot-shaped but creamy in colour. Turnips are white, too, or yellow, in which case they are swedes. We like parsnips; turnips, we're not so sure about. We know we want parsnips here and think you will, too. ■ SERVES 6

4 medium baking potatoes, peeled, diced, and placed in cold water to cover

2 tablespoons olive oil

2 large parsnips, peeled and diced

2 large carrots, peeled and diced

salt and freshly ground black pepper to taste

chopped fresh parsley for garnish

Pat the potatoes dry with kitchen paper.

Heat the oil in a large frying pan over high heat until hot. Add the potatoes and cook, tossing, for 8 minutes. Add the parsnips, carrots, salt, pepper and 125ml (4fl oz) of water. Cover the pan and lower the heat to medium-high. Braise the vegetables for 15 minutes, until just tender when tested with a fork.

Serve with plenty of fresh parsley on top.

Yam Gratin

If you want to go all out, serve this grand but so very comforting gratin with Danny Aiello's New York Sirloin Steak and his Cherokee Indian Curry AAA Steak Sauce (page 65) and Caramelized East Indian Vegetables (page 162) for a special dinner.

You can also serve this to good effect with something as simple as roast chicken. ■ SERVES 6

3 large yams, peeled and sliced paper-thin

3 tablespoons chopped garlic

2 tablespoons chopped fresh marjoram or 1 tablespoon dried

salt and freshly ground black pepper to taste

250g (8oz) fat-free Monterey Jack or Cheddar cheese, grated, or a combination of both

50g (2oz) Parmesan cheese, freshly grated

250ml (8fl oz) double cream

4 tablespoons unsalted butter at room temperature

Preheat the oven to 200°C, 400°F, gas mark 6. Lightly butter a 32 x 23cm (13 x 9in) gratin dish.

Arrange ⅓ of the yam slices in overlapping rows on the bottom of the prepared dish. Sprinkle on ⅓ of the garlic and marjoram, and season with salt and pepper. Sprinkle with ⅓ of the Monterey Jack and Parmesan, then pour ⅓ of the cream over all. Dot with ⅓ of the butter. Press the slices down slightly with a metal spatula.

Make 2 more layers in the same way, ending with a dusting of Parmesan.

Cover the dish with foil and bake for 50 minutes. Remove the foil and bake for 5–10 minutes more to brown the top lightly.

Serve the gratin hot, either cut into squares or spooned from the dish.

Sandy Austin's Brown Rice Salad
Joanne is particularly fond of this dish because of the whole-grain base. It goes beautifully with Caroline's Southern-Fried Chicken (page 84). ■ SERVES 6 TO 10

500g (1lb) brown rice
juice and zest of 1 orange
3 spring onions, thinly sliced crosswise
750g (1½lb) black or green seedless
    grapes, stemmed
150g (5oz) whole almonds, toasted

DRESSING
15g (½oz) root ginger, peeled
1½ tablespoons cider vinegar

1½ tablespoons brown sugar
2 tablespoons champagne vinegar
125ml (4fl oz) olive oil
125ml (4fl oz) vegetable oil
⅛ teaspoon ground nutmeg
salt to taste
1 teaspoon freshly ground black
    pepper
2 tablespoons toasted and ground
    coriander seeds

Blend the dressing ingredients in a food processor or blender until emulsified.

In a large saucepan, boil the rice in salted water until tender. Drain immediately. Place the hot rice in a large bowl. Stir in the dressing, orange juice and zest and spring onions. Leave to cool.

Adjust the seasonings to taste and add more oil if needed. Fold in the grapes and almonds, and toss well.

Last spring my husband and I were enjoying the beach on Siesta Key (Sarasota, Florida). A group of young musicians had the apartment below us for the week. . . .

By the third day they were very red and very miserable. . . . Reaching for my trusty bottle of Paul Newman Vinegar and Oil, I said, "Try rubbing this all over!" They did, and it worked—honest! They even wrote a song about it: "Rub it on, cool it off."

SINCERELY YOURS,
A.

Butch's Wild West Tex-Mex Salad

To showcase the flavours of the Southwest, Cindy Kovar created a colourful and flavourful salad. This perfect make-ahead side dish walked away with the 1996 grand prize. Chipotle chillies in adobo sauce add big flavour—Texas style! They are available in the Spanish food section in most grocery stores or in specialty food stores. Cindy donated her award to the 100 Pennies Scholarship Drive.

SERVES 6 AS A MAIN DISH OR 12 AS AN ACCOMPANIMENT

DRESSING

250ml (8fl oz) Newman's Own Olive Oil and Vinegar Dressing, or your favourite
4 tablespoons red wine vinegar
3 tablespoons chipotle chillies in adobo sauce, chopped
juice of 1 large lime (about 2 tablespoons)
1 tablespoon ground cumin
2 teaspoons salt

SALAD

three 490–575g (15½–19oz) cans black beans, rinsed and drained
four 490–500g (15½–16oz) cans sweetcorn, drained
500g (1lb) cooked white rice
75g (3oz) finely chopped red onion
2 spring onions, finely chopped
4 tablespoons chopped coriander

500g (1lb) tomatoes, coarsely chopped
lime wedges and coriander sprigs for garnish

To make the dressing, mix all the ingredients together well in a bowl.

To make the salad, mix all the salad ingredients in a large bowl.

Add the dressing to the salad, toss, cover and place in the refrigerator for at least 1 hour or up to 1 day.

Before serving the salad, add the chopped tomatoes and garnish with the lime wedges and coriander sprigs.

Breads and Snacks

Jalapeño Spoon Bread ▪ **Cornmeal Squares with Salsa** ▪ **Nell Newman's Whole Wheat Raisin Scones** ▪ **Joanne's Courgette Bread** ▪ **Nell's Sesame Loaves** ▪ **Joanne's Cereal** ▪ **Newman's Munchies** ▪ **Paul's Picture Show Popcorn Crunch** ▪ **'Pops' Newman's Coffee-Toffee Macadamia Crunch**

Jalapeño Spoon Bread

This Southwest-style spoon bread is tailor-made for serving with Harry Belafonte's Pork, Apple and Yam Salad (page 73). If you don't have a large cast-iron frying pan, bake it in an 28 x 23cm (11 x 9in) baking tin. Be sure to serve it warm. ■ SERVES 6

225g (7½oz) yellow cornmeal

40g (1½oz) flour

750ml (1¼ pints) semi-skimmed or full-cream milk

125g (4oz) unsalted butter, melted

½ teaspoon salt

4 egg yolks

2 teaspoons baking powder

25g (1oz) frozen sweetcorn, defrosted

2 tablespoons julienned basil leaves

1 jalapeño or serrano chilli, seeded and diced

1 tablespoon freshly ground black pepper

2 egg whites at room temperature

Preheat the oven to 180°C, 350°F, gas mark 4. Generously butter a 30cm (12in) cast-iron frying pan.

Sift the cornmeal and flour together in a bowl.

In a medium saucepan, bring 475ml (16fl oz) of the milk just to the boil. Add the cornmeal mixture gradually, whisking it in vigorously. Stir in the butter and salt. Cook over medium heat for 2 minutes, then transfer to a bowl and leave to cool to room temperature.

Beat the egg yolks with an electric mixer until they form a ribbon when the beater is lifted. Stir into the cooled cornmeal mixture with the baking powder and the remaining 250ml (8fl oz) of milk. Stir in the corn, basil, chilli and black pepper, and combine well.

Beat the egg whites with the electric mixer and clean beaters until stiff but not dry. Fold into the cornmeal batter until fully incorporated.

Scrape the batter into the prepared pan and level the top. Bake for 30–40 minutes, or until a knife inserted in the centre comes out clean.

Serve warm, in wedges.

Dear Sir:

Recently after reading about some of the research on hot spicy foods . . . I decided to try some of your salsa sauce. I now eat your salsa several times per week and have experienced a clearing of the lung congestion that has troubled me for years. . . . It was amazing the results after a few days of eating cheese and crackers topped with your salsa—my left lung is now as clear as a bell. . . .

SINCERELY YOURS,
J.B.

Cornmeal Squares with Salsa

Salsa, mild, medium or hot, makes a surefire topping for these grilled cornmeal squares with chillies, cheese and coriander. Staying in the southwestern mode, serve as a bread with chilli. These are also good with soup and/or a main-course salad.

■ MAKES 15 SQUARES ■ SERVES 4 TO 6

150g (5oz) yellow cornmeal
1 teaspoon chilli powder
1 teaspoon salt
125g (4oz) Monterey Jack or Cheddar cheese, grated
one 125g (4oz) can green chillies, drained, chopped and patted dry

2 tablespoons chopped coriander
6 tablespoons vegetable oil
one 325g (11oz) jar Newman's Own All-Natural Bandito Salsa, or your favourite

Oil a 37 x 25 x 1cm (15 x 10 x ½in) baking tin.

Combine the cornmeal and chilli powder in a small bowl.

In a large saucepan, bring 1 litre (1¾ pints) of water and the salt to the boil over medium heat. Sprinkle the cornmeal mixture, 25g (1oz) at a time, into the water, whisking constantly. Cook, stirring constantly with a wooden spoon, until thickened, about 10 minutes. Stir in the cheese, chillies and coriander. Spread the batter evenly in the prepared baking tin and refrigerate until cooled completely.

Cut the cold corn bread into 15 squares, each 7 x 8.5cm (3 x 3½ in). In a large nonstick frying pan, heat 2 tablespoons of the oil over medium-high heat. Place 5 squares in the skillet and cook, turning once, until golden brown, about 8–10 minutes. Transfer to a plate.

Cook the remaining squares, in batches of 5, in the same way with the remaining oil.

Serve the corn bread squares warm with the salsa as a topping.

Nell Newman's Wholewheat Raisin Scones

While in England one spring, I managed to get a recipe for this traditional teatime treat from a family friend. Her scones were made with white flour and sugar, which I have changed to wholewheat and honey as a matter of personal preference. They can be made either way or somewhere in between; white flour makes lighter scones. This is best served at teatime with heavy doses of butter and jam. ■ MAKES 8 TO 12

125g (4oz) unsalted butter
4 tablespoons honey
250g (8oz) wholewheat flour

75ml (3fl oz) milk
3 teaspoons baking soda
40g (1½oz) raisins

Preheat the oven to 180°C, 350°F, gas mark 4. Grease a baking sheet well, then flour it lightly.

In a medium bowl, combine the butter, honey and flour with your hands until it resembles coarse breadcrumbs. Stir in the milk, baking soda and raisins until well mixed and a doughy ball forms.

Lightly flour the work surface and the top of the dough ball. Roll the dough evenly in all directions until it is 1.5–2.5cm (¾–1in) thick. Using the rim of a glass or a biscuit-cutter with a diameter of 5–6cm (2–2½ in), cut out individual scones and place on the prepared baking sheet. Bake for 20–30 minutes, or until browned on top.

The scones can be served hot out of the oven or cold.

Joanne's Courgette Bread

This is good for breakfast, as an accompaniment to a bowl of soup for lunch, or with a cup of coffee or tea as a snack. ▪ **MAKES 2 LOAVES**

375g (12oz) plain flour	**3 eggs**
1 teaspoon baking soda	**250g (8oz) sugar**
1 teaspoon baking powder	**250ml (8fl oz) vegetable oil**
1 teaspoon ground cinnamon	**1 teaspoon vanilla extract**
1 teaspoon salt	**2 large courgettes, grated**

Preheat the oven to 180°C, 350°F, gas mark 4. Grease well 2 loaf tins, measuring 21.5 x 11 x 6cm (8½ x 4½ x 2½ in).

Sift together the flour, baking soda, baking powder, cinnamon and salt.

In a large bowl, beat the eggs until foamy. Add the sugar, oil, vanilla extract and dry ingredients, a little at a time. The batter will be thick. Add the courgettes–the mixture will be sticky.

Pour the batter into the prepared loaf tins and bake for 1 hour. Check after 50 minutes. If a toothpick comes out clean, the bread is done.

Great served warm or cold. The loaves may be frozen.

Nell's Sesame Loaves

My family is quite fond of this wonderful recipe. Consequently, it doesn't last long in our household, especially since it goes so well with soups, salads or sandwiches such as Caroline Murphy's Tuna Salad (page 115). I would love to lie and say it is my original creation, but I must give credit where credit is due. This recipe was given to me by family friend, and professional cook, Cary Bell of Bar Harbor, Maine.

MAKES 2 LOAVES

250ml (8fl oz) boiling water
60g (3½oz) instant rolled oats
125g (4oz) unhulled sesame seeds
350ml (12fl oz) warm water
1 teaspoon dried yeast

1 teaspoon sugar or honey
500g (1lb) wholewheat flour
1 teaspoon salt
1 handful cornmeal

In a bowl, mix together the boiling water, oats and sesame seeds. Leave to cool.

In a large bowl, combine the warm water, yeast and sugar. Put the bowl in a warm place. When the yeast mixture is bubbly (5–15 minutes), add the flour, salt and sesame mixture and work until the dough forms a ball. (This may require a bit more flour.)

Flour the work surface as well as your hands and the dough. Transfer the dough to the floured surface and knead well for 10–15 minutes. Leave to rise for 45 minutes.

While the dough is rising, preheat the oven to 180°C, 350°F, gas mark 4. Grease 2 long, shallow baking tins or a baking sheet and sprinkle with the cornmeal.

Knead the dough again and shape it into 2 long loaves. Place the loaves in the prepared tins, or on the baking sheet and bake for 30–50 minutes, until golden brown and hollow-sounding when tapped on the bottom with a wooden spoon or your fingers.

Joanne's Cereal

Joanne's culinary repertoire is limited, but she makes up in quality what she lacks in quantity. Her breakfast cereal is the best way for anyone to start the day, and it would certainly become a Newman's Own product if it weren't for the complicated process required to create it. It is best to make a large batch of the cereal, which can then be kept in the refrigerator for several weeks. You will need to bake this in batches; the recipe will fill 3–4 baking sheets. ■ MAKES LOTS

300ml (½ pint) vegetable oil
1kg (2lb) honey
500g (1lb) rolled oats
1kg (2lb) almonds
500g (1lb) sunflower seeds

50g (2oz) sesame seeds
125g (4oz) chopped cashews
125g (4oz) chopped walnuts
250g (8oz) wheatgerm, roasted

Preheat the oven to 160°C, 325°F, gas mark 3.

Mix the oil and honey together with 350ml (12fl oz) of water. Mix together the dry ingredients and combine with the honey mixture. Spread thinly on nonstick baking sheets. Bake and keep turning until golden brown, about 20–30 minutes. Cool and keep in tins.

Newman's Munchies

Mary Jane Bennett used a triple play of pretzels, popcorn and Caesar dressing teamed with mixed nuts and spices to create a savoury snack. Prepare the recipe ahead. Store in airtight containers to take to your next sporting event. Mary Jane, a 1996 runner-up, donated her award to the San Diego chapter of the Achievement Rewards for College Scientists. ■ MAKES ABOUT 11 CUPS

125g (4oz) Newman's Own Second Generation Organic Pretzel Sticks, or your favourite, broken in half
250g (8oz) whole nuts (dry-roasted unsalted cashews, macadamia nuts, pecans or walnuts; peanuts are too small)
3 tablespoons Newman's Own Caesar Dressing, or your favourite

½ teaspoon dried basil
½ teaspoon dried oregano
4 tablespoons grated Parmesan cheese
2 bags popped Newman's Own All-Natural Butter Flavor Oldstyle Picture Show Microwave Popcorn, or your favourite, prepared according to the package directions

Preheat the oven to 150°C, 300°F, gas mark 2.

Place the pretzels and nuts in a 32 x 23cm (13 x 9in) metal baking tin. Combine the dressing, basil and oregano and pour over the pretzels and nuts. Sprinkle 2 tablespoons of the cheese over all and mix to coat. Bake for 20–30 minutes, stirring once.

Pour half of the popcorn into a large bowl and sprinkle with 1 tablespoon of the cheese. Pour the remaining popcorn into the bowl and sprinkle with the remaining tablespoon of cheese. Add the baked pretzels and nuts, mix, and serve.

Dear Mr. Newman:

My 92-year-old dad likes popcorn but had to give it up because of the hulls getting under his dentures. I gave him a handful of your popcorn, and the first bite was followed by "Hey, that melts in your mouth." Took out his dentures and showed me—clean as a whistle.

THANKS,
W.S.

Paul's Picture Show Popcorn Crunch

This sweet and nutty snack is the creation of Jane Skvarca, a 1994 finalist. Her award was donated to the Day Nursery and the Assistance League of Antelope Valley.

■ MAKES ABOUT 13 CUPS

125g (4oz) whole almonds
125g (4oz) pecan halves
125g (4oz) cashews or walnuts
1 bag Newman's Own Oldstyle Picture Show Microwave Popcorn, or your favourite

125g (4oz) margarine
125g (4oz) unsalted butter
315g (10½oz) sugar
4 tablespoons light corn syrup
1 tablespoon pure vanilla extract

Preheat the oven to 150°C, 300°F, gas mark 2. Grease a large heatproof mixing bowl and a 37 x 25cm (15 x 10in) baking tin with margarine.

In another 37 x 25cm (15 x 10in) baking tin, combine the almonds, pecans and cashews, and toast in the oven for 20 minutes, stirring occasionally. Remove the pan from the oven and cool the nuts to room temperature.

Pop the popcorn following the package directions. Pour the popcorn into the prepared bowl. Add the nuts and mix well.

Melt the margarine and butter in a heavy saucepan over medium heat. Add the sugar, corn syrup and 4 tablespoons of water. Mix well and stir often. Continue to cook over medium-high heat until it reaches 140°C, 275°F on a sugar thermometer. Remove the pan from the heat and slowly stir in the vanilla extract. (Stir carefully because the vanilla extract will spatter when added to the hot syrup.)

Pour the hot syrup over the popcorn-nut mixture and mix until evenly coated. Immediately pour the popcorn into the prepared baking tin. Leave to cool for 1 hour. Break into pieces and store in an airtight container.

'Pops' Newman's Coffee-Toffee Macadamia Crunch

For Bob Gadsby, a love for popcorn as a child developed into an art form as a bachelor. Even though his wife is now queen of the kitchen, popcorn is one area where he reigns supreme. His 1996 prize-winning recipe combines popcorn with rich, buttery macadamia nuts and just a hint of coffee. Bob donated his award to the Boundary County Library and the Volunteer Fire Department. ▪ MAKES ABOUT 13 CUPS

One 90g (3½oz) bag Newman's Own All-Natural Flavor Oldstyle Picture Show Microwave Popcorn, or your favourite

250g (8oz) macadamia nuts, coarsely chopped

175g (6oz) unsalted butter or margarine

250g (8oz) sugar

75g (3oz) light brown sugar

4 tablespoons coffee-flavoured liqueur or strong coffee

4 tablespoons light corn syrup

2 teaspoons vanilla extract

Butter a large roasting tin.

Pop the popcorn according to the package directions. Pour into the prepared tin and add the macadamia nuts. Toss to mix.

In a large saucepan, combine the butter, sugar, brown sugar, liqueur and corn syrup, and bring to the boil over medium heat, stirring constantly. Continue cooking and stirring until the mixture reaches 145°C, 290°F on a sugar thermometer. Remove the pan from the heat and stir in the vanilla extract. Pour over the popcorn mixture and stir until evenly coated.

Cool until firm and break into pieces.

Store in an airtight container.

Desserts

Lemonade Torte for a Long Hot Summer ▪ Sockarooni Orange Kiss-Me Cake ▪ Tropical Coconut Tapioca Pudding ▪ Julia Roberts's Fresh Peach Crisp ▪ Fresh Fruits with Sour Cream Sauce ▪ Dried Cranberry and Apple Caramel Custard ▪ Raspberry Napoleons with Lemon Whipped Cream ▪ Melanie Griffith's Macadamia, Chocolate Chip and Peanut Butter Mini-Turnovers ▪ Cy Coleman's Potstickers with Cream Cheese and Strawberry Filling ▪ Almond Fruit Pudding

The good thing about excesses is that you can't get too much of them.

—STOLEN FROM AN UNKNOWN POET BY BANDITO NEWMAN, 1985

Lemonade Torte for a Long Hot Summer

The inspiration to create this 1995 finalist recipe derived from the love of Marta Rallis-Lagreco's family for a particular chocolate torte. Marta donated her prize money to the Guide Dog Institute of America, the Gray Panthers, and HART Muttmatchers. ■ SERVES 8

90g (3½oz) blanched almonds
375g (12oz) sugar
75g (3oz) wholewheat breadcrumbs
¼ teaspoon baking powder
¼ teaspoon ground cinnamon
1 tablespoon grated lemon zest

6 large egg whites
250ml (8fl oz) Newman's Own Old-Fashioned Roadside Virgin Lemonade, or your favourite
2 tablespoons icing sugar

Preheat the oven to 180°C, 350°F, gas mark 4. Butter and flour a 23cm (9in) spring-form pan.

In a food processor, grind the almonds with 250g (8oz) of the sugar. In a medium bowl, mix the ground almond mixture with the breadcrumbs, baking powder, cinnamon and lemon zest.

In a large bowl, beat the egg whites and the remaining sugar with an electric mixer on high speed until stiff peaks form. Gently fold the crumb mixture into the beaten egg whites. Pour the mixture into the prepared springform pan and bake on the lower oven rack for 1 hour.

Put the lemonade in a saucepan over medium-high heat for 10 minutes, until reduced by half.

Remove the torte from the oven. Pour the reduced lemonade gradually over the top of the hot torte. Let the torte stand in the pan on a wire rack until cool.

To serve, remove the sides of the springform pan and dust the top of the torte with the icing sugar.

Sockarooni Orange Kiss-Me Cake

No one will ever guess the secret ingredient in this sweet and tangy cake, which secured a 1997 runner-up prize for Kim Landhuis. Kim donated her award to the Fort Dodge Public Library and the Fort Dodge United Way. ■ SERVES 12

2 large eggs
250ml (8fl oz) Newman's Own
    Sockarooni Spaghetti Sauce, or
    your favourite
175ml (6fl oz) freshly squeezed orange
    juice
125ml (4fl oz) vegetable oil
375g (12oz) plain flour
375g (12oz) sugar
2 teaspoons pumpkin pie spice
1½ teaspoons baking powder
1½ teaspoons baking soda
250g (8oz) sultanas

125g (4oz) chopped almonds

FROSTING

175g (6oz) low-fat cream cheese,
    softened
25g (1oz) unsalted butter or margarine,
    softened
4 tablespoons freshly squeezed orange
    juice
½ teaspoon grated orange zest
500g (1lb) icing sugar
3 maraschino cherries, halved
18 almond slivers

Preheat the oven to 180°C, 350°F, gas mark 4. Grease a 25cm (10in) tube cake tin.

In a large bowl, beat the eggs until combined and add the sauce, orange juice and oil. Mix well.

In a large bowl, combine the flour, sugar, pumpkin pie spice, baking powder and baking soda. Beat the mixture slowly into the egg mixture. Stir in the raisins and almonds. Pour the batter into the prepared tin and bake for 40–50 minutes, or until a toothpick inserted in the centre comes out clean. Cool the cake on a rack for 15 minutes, then remove from the tin and cool completely.

To make the frosting, in a large bowl, beat the cream cheese together with the butter, orange juice and orange peel. Add the icing sugar gradually, beating until smooth.

Spread the frosting on the cake. On the top, make 6 flower decorations by surrounding each cherry half with 3 almond slivers.

Tropical Coconut Tapioca Pudding

This is a new spin on tapioca pudding, made here with coconut milk and topped with a fresh fruit and yogurt sauce. Tapioca comes in different sizes; you want the small pearl variety. ▪ SERVES 6

TAPIOCA

130g (4½oz) small pearl tapioca
400ml (14fl oz) unsweetened coconut milk
250ml (8fl oz) milk
60g (2½oz) sugar
1 egg, lightly beaten
1 teaspoon vanilla extract

TOPPING

50g (2oz) fresh blueberries
60g (2½oz) fresh raspberries
50g (2oz) finely chopped fresh pineapple
1 banana, thinly sliced
40g (1½oz) dark brown sugar
175g (6oz) vanilla yogurt

To make the tapioca, in a medium saucepan, combine the tapioca, coconut milk, milk, sugar and egg over medium heat, stirring to dissolve the sugar. Bring to the boil and simmer, stirring constantly, for 30 minutes, or until the tapioca pearls are soft. Remove the pan from the heat and stir in the vanilla extract. Pour the tapioca into a shallow bowl. Place clingfilm directly on the surface of the tapioca (to prevent a skin from forming) and leave to cool.

To make the topping, place all the ingredients in a bowl and stir gently to combine. Cover and refrigerate until serving time.

Serve the tapioca with a generous amount of topping.

Julia Roberts's Fresh Peach Crisp

What sets this crisp apart is its topping: it is crusty and wonderful, and there is lots of it. If unpeeled peaches bother you, peel them. Serve this for dessert, of course, and also for breakfast. ■ SERVES 6

7 ripe but firm peaches, unpeeled,
    stoned and coarsely chopped
4 tablespoons fresh lemon juice
4 tablespoons whisky
50g (2oz) sugar
40g (1½oz) dark brown sugar
50g (2oz) unsalted butter
softened frozen vanilla yogurt as an
    accompaniment

TOPPING
300g (10oz) flour
75g (3oz) dark brown sugar
1 teaspoon ground cinnamon
375g (12oz) unsalted butter, melted

Preheat the oven to 180°C, 350°F, gas mark 4. Butter a 32 x 23x 5cm (13 x 9 x 2in) baking dish.

In a large bowl, toss the peaches together with the lemon juice. Add the whisky, sugar and brown sugar and combine well. Spread the mixture on the bottom of the baking dish and dot with small pieces of the butter.

Make the topping. In a bowl, stir together the flour, brown sugar and cinnamon until combined. Add the butter gradually, stirring it in to form a crumbly mixture. Sprinkle it evenly over the peaches. Even though the topping should be evenly distributed, you want a rustic, pebbly look to the top.

Cover the dish with foil and bake for 40 minutes. Uncover and bake for 5–10 minutes more to brown the top.

Leave to cool slightly, then serve warm in bowls, topped with scoops of frozen yogurt.

Fresh Fruits with Sour Cream Sauce

You don't have to use lots of this sauce to get its full marvellous effect. Assorted fresh berries are a natural with it, too. Or spoon a little of it over cake.

If you're looking for something really special, make the Raspberry Napoleons on page 196, and instead of dusting the plates for serving with icing sugar, spoon a small pool of this sauce on the bottom of each plate, then place a Napoleon in the centre. ■ SERVES 6

375g (12oz) sliced fresh fruits, such as
banana, mango, papaya and kiwi
350ml (12fl oz) sour cream
50g (2oz) dark brown sugar

juice of 1 lemon
1 teaspoon finely chopped fresh mint
plus mint sprigs for garnish
(optional)

Keep the fruit chilled until ready to serve.

In a bowl, combine the sour cream, brown sugar, lemon juice and mint, and stir together until the sugar is dissolved. Pour the sauce into a serving bowl, cover, and chill until ready to serve.

Serve the fruit decorated with the mint sprigs and pass the sour cream sauce as a topping. Serve with crisp biscuits.

Dear Sirs:

I am writing you this letter in regard to Newman's Own Virgin Lemonade. I am an auctioneer and on occasion while working my throat will get dry and have phlegm in it and makes me get hoarse. When the above happens and I get hoarse, nothing else will cut this phlegm and dryness except this Virgin Lemonade—it cuts through and cleans up my hoarseness. You should put it on the bottle—cuts through phlegm.

THANK YOU VERY MUCH,
L.E.

Dried Cranberry and Apple Caramel Custard

Most custards are made with double cream or milk mixed together with eggs; this unusual version uses lemonade in place of dairy products. ▪ SERVES 6

CARAMEL

175g (6oz) sugar
3½ tablespoons water

APPLES

90g (2½oz) unsalted butter
4–5 large tart apples, peeled and sliced
4 tablespoons Newman's Own Old-Fashioned Roadside Virgin Lemonade
90g (2½oz) sugar

½ teaspoon ground cinnamon
75g (3oz) dried cranberries

APPLE CUSTARD

4 eggs
4 tablespoons Newman's Own Old-Fashioned Roadside Virgin Lemonade, or your favourite
2 tablespoons Grand Marnier (optional)

icing sugar for decoration

To make the caramel, in a small, heavy saucepan swirl the sugar and water together over medium heat until the sugar has dissolved and the liquid is clear. Bring the mixture to the boil and with a brush dipped in cold water constantly brush down the sugar crystals that form on the sides of the pan. Cook, without stirring, until the sugar syrup turns caramel brown in colour. Immediately pour the hot syrup very carefully into a 1.5 litre (2½ pint) ovenproof mould and turn it to coat the bottom and sides.

Prepare the apples. In a large, heavy frying pan melt the butter over medium heat. Add the apple slices and toss until coated with the butter. Add the lemonade, sugar, cinnamon and cranberries and stir to combine. Cover the pan and cook the apples for about 5 minutes, until soft but still holding their shape. Remove the pan from the heat and leave to cool.

Preheat the oven to 180°C, 350°F, gas mark 4.

To make the custard, in a large bowl beat the eggs together with the lemonade and Grand Marnier. Fold in the apple slices and any cooking juices from the pan. Turn the mixture into the caramelized ovenproof mould.

Place the mould in a large roasting tin and pour enough hot water into the tin to come about halfway up the sides of the mould. Bake for about 1½ hours, or until the custard shrinks slightly away from the sides. Remove from the oven. Take the mould out of the roasting tin and leave to stand for 15 minutes. Unmould onto a serving plate.

Sprinkle the icing sugar over the top and serve hot.

Raspberry Napoleons with Lemon Whipped Cream

Classic Napoleons are notoriously difficult to make, but frozen puff pastry and a whipped cream filling make all the difference here. These luscious pastries cannot be assembled too far in advance, though—no more than thirty minutes before serving time. You want to keep all the textures intact.

If these are not luxurious enough (and they are), there's a way to make them even more so: serve in a pool of the brown sugar sour cream sauce on page 192. ■ **SERVES 6**

two 530g (17¼oz) packs frozen puff pastry (3 sheets) defrosted according to the directions (reserve the remaining sheet for another time)
350ml (12fl oz) cold double cream

1 tablespoon icing sugar, plus extra for decoration
½ teaspoon lemon extract
freshly grated zest of 1 lemon
three 300ml (½ pint) packs of raspberries
6 mint sprigs for decoration

Preheat the oven to 230°C, 450°F, gas mark 8. Have ready 4 heavy-duty baking sheets. Line 3 of them with baking parchment.

Working with 1 sheet of puff pastry at a time, spread the pastry sheet evenly over 1 of the baking sheets. With a sharp knife, cut it into 6 pieces, and cover with another lined baking sheet. Spread a second sheet of pastry over the baking sheet, cut it into 6 pieces, and cover with the third baking sheet. Top with the remaining sheet of pastry, cut it into 6 pieces and top with the last baking sheet. Transfer the stacked baking sheets to the oven and bake for 15–20 minutes. Carefully lift up the top baking sheet to check the colour of the pastry. It should be deep golden brown. If not, return the stack to the oven. Check every 5 minutes until the pastry is golden brown. Remove the stack from the oven, remove the top baking sheet and allow the pastry to cool.

In a large chilled bowl, beat the cream, sugar and lemon extract with an electric mixer until soft peaks form. It should not be stiff but should fall softly from the beater in mounds. Stir in the zest. Cover and chill until it is time to assemble the dessert.

To assemble the Napoleons, dust 6 dessert plates generously with icing sugar. Place a piece of pastry on 1 plate and top with about 2–3 tablespoons of whipped cream. Top with a small handful of berries and another piece of pastry. Add another layer of whipped cream and raspberries, and end with a third piece of pastry.

Make 5 more Napoleons in the same way.

To serve, dust the tops of the Napoleons with icing sugar and decorate each with a mint sprig. Serve immediately. The pastry is at its very best still flaky and crisp.

Melanie Griffith's Macadamia, Chocolate Chip and Peanut Butter Mini-Turnovers

Macadamia nuts make the peanut butter filling in these turnovers unforgettable. It is a little like having a mini–candy bar wrapped in a puff pastry case. When you feel the urge coming on for these, there's an easy solution: prepare a full batch, then freeze some of them. They freeze beautifully, we are glad to say.

■ **MAKES 32 MINI-TURNOVERS**

one 340g (11½oz) jar smooth peanut butter, at room temperature
50g (2oz) milk chocolate chips
125g (4oz) macadamia nuts, toasted and chopped
one 530g (17½oz) pack frozen puff pastry (2 sheets), defrosted according to the pack directions

1 egg, lightly beaten
icing sugar for decoration (optional)
mint sprigs for decoration (optional)
vanilla ice cream as an accompaniment

Preheat the oven to 220°C, 425°F, gas mark 7.

In a bowl, stir together the peanut butter, chocolate chips and macadamia nuts until well combined.

Work with 1 sheet of puff pastry at a time. Lightly flour a work surface. Lay 1 sheet of puff pastry on the surface and gently roll it out in all directions to thin it slightly. With a sharp knife, cut the sheet into quarters, then cut each quarter into quarters, making 16 pieces in total.

Place 1 teaspoon of the nut filling in the centre of each piece of pastry. Fold the pastry on the diagonal to form a triangle. Press the open edges of the pastry to seal. (At this point the turnovers can be frozen. Arrange in layers, separated by sheets of greaseproof paper, in a freezer container.) Brush the top of the turnover with the beaten egg and place on a baking sheet.

Make the remaining mini-turnovers in the same way and brush with the beaten egg.

Bake for 15 minutes. If the turnovers are frozen, preheat the oven to 240°C, 475°F, gas mark 9. Bake the pastries on the baking sheet for 5 minutes. Lower the heat to 200°C, 400°F, gas mark 9 and bake for 15 minutes.

Serve at once, dusted with icing sugar and decorated with a mint sprig, with the ice cream.

Cy Coleman's Potstickers with Cream Cheese and Strawberry Filling

Serve these dessert potstickers warm and the tropical fruit salsa well chilled.

Use either gyoza or wonton wrappers to make these. You'll have leftover wrappers; freeze them in an airtight container because you'll want to make these again. ■ **MAKES ABOUT 36 POTSTICKERS**

FILLING

250g (8oz) strawberries, sliced
125g (4oz) sugar
4 tablespoons fresh lemon juice
1 tablespoon Grand Marnier
250g (8oz) whipped cream cheese

SALSA

150g (5oz) strawberries, chopped
150g (5oz) papaya, chopped
150g (5oz) mango, chopped
4 tablespoons julienned mint leaves
2 tablespoons fresh orange juice

1 tablespoon kirsch
1 tablespoon sugar

one 375g (12oz) packet gyoza
    wrappers or wonton skins
cornflour for baking sheet
vegetable oil for cooking

softened frozen vanilla yogurt
icing sugar for decoration (optional)
fresh mint sprigs for decoration

To make the filling, combine the strawberries, sugar, lemon juice and Grand Marnier in an enamel saucepan. Cook over medium heat, stirring every now and then, until the liquid is evaporated, about 5 minutes. Leave to cool completely, then stir into the cream cheese until blended.

To make the salsa, stir the fruit, mint leaves, orange juice, kirsch, sugar and 2 tablespoons of water together in a bowl. Cover and refrigerate until needed.

Sprinkle a baking sheet with cornflour. Preheat the oven to 120°C, 250°F, gas mark ½.

Make one potsticker at a time by placing ½ teaspoon of the filling in the middle of the wrapper. Brush the edges of the wrapper with water and fold over, making either half moons or rectangles. Press the edges together to seal. (A small amount of the filling may seep out of the sides; wipe off with damp kitchen paper.) Brush the filled potstickers very lightly with cornflour and place in a single layer on the prepared baking sheet, leaving space between them. The cornflour helps to keep the wrappers from sticking. (The potstickers can be frozen at this point. Arrange in layers, separated by sheets of greaseproof paper, in foil freezer containers.)

Heat ½ teaspoon of oil in a cast-iron frying pan until hot. Cook in batches of 6 over medium heat, 1½ minutes on each side, until golden brown. Turn and cook for 1½ minutes on the other side, until golden brown. Transfer to a baking sheet and keep warm in the preheated oven.

To serve, divide the salsa among 6 dessert plates, spreading it to the edges. Put 6 warm potstickers per plate in a circle on the salsa, leaving the centre of the circle open. Place a scoop of yogurt in the middle. Sprinkle with icing sugar and decorate with the mint sprigs.

Cy Coleman at the 1995 camp gala

Almond Fruit Pudding

Try this with all the fruits suggested below, or with only one or two of them. Either way, it is an especially good dessert for winter, warming but not heavy. If you want to dress it up a bit, scatter on the top a few fresh mint sprigs and dried berries that you've soaked in kirsch. ■ SERVES 4 TO 6

250g (8oz) dried fruit such as cherries, blueberries, blackberries and cranberries
250g (8oz) sugar
175ml (6fl oz) Newman's Own Old-Fashioned Roadside Virgin Lemonade, or your favourite

5 eggs
125g (4oz) ground blanched almonds
½ teaspoon almond extract

Preheat the oven to 180°C, 350°F, gas mark 4.

In a saucepan, simmer the dried fruit with 75g (3oz) of the sugar and the lemonade until the fruit is tender and the liquid is nearly absorbed, about 4 minutes. Drain if necessary. Place the fruit in a 1.5–2 litre (2½–3½ pint) soufflé dish.

In a large bowl, beat the eggs until thick and lemon-coloured. Gradually beat in the remaining sugar, 1 tablespoon at a time. Fold in the almonds and almond extract. Pour the mixture over the fruit in the soufflé dish and bake for 45–50 minutes, or until set.

Serve hot.

Mr. Newman:

Last night my girlfriend treated me to a fabulous meal. It was quick and easy and quite good. . . .

During dinner my girlfriend mentioned you were a movie star. I would be interested to know what you've made. If you act as well as you cook, your movies would be worth watching.

KEEP UP THE GOOD WORK,
M.

P.S. Are any of your movies in VCR?

What I like is when life wiggles its hips and throws me a surprise. All the experts said we couldn't produce these foods without chemical preservatives; they said we couldn't use fresh garlic and onions; they said we had to advertise; they said no business in the world could give away 100 percent of its profits. Well, we didn't listen to any of 'em, and just look at us. I feel that spreading our products around is spreading the gospel, and I'll stay at it as long as I enjoy it—and, as of now, I'm having a fine time.

—PAUL NEWMAN

Index

Metric Equivalents

Liquid and Dry Measure Equivalents

CUSTOMARY	METRIC
¼ teaspoon	1.25 milliliters
½ teaspoon	2.5 milliliters
1 teaspoon	5 milliliters
1 tablespoon	15 milliliters
1 fluid ounce	30 milliliters
¼ cup	60 milliliters
⅓ cup	80 milliliters
½ cup	120 milliliters
1 cup	240 milliliters
1 pint (2 cups)	480 milliliters
1 quart (4 cups, 32 ounces)	960 milliliters (.96 liters)
1 gallon (4 quarts)	3.84 liters
1 ounce (by weight)	25 grams
¼ pound (4 ounces)	125 grams
1 pound (16 ounces)	500 grams
2.2 pounds	1 kilogram (1,000 grams)

Oven Temperature Equivalents

DESCRIPTION	FAHRENHEIT	CELSIUS
Cool	200	90
Very slow	250	120
Slow	300–325	150–160
Moderately slow	325–350	160–180
Moderate	350–375	180–190
Moderately hot	375–400	190–200
Hot	400–450	200–230
Very hot	450–500	230–260

About the Authors

Paul Newman is probably best known for his spectacularly successful food conglomerate. In addition to giving the profits to charity, he also ran Frank Sinatra out of the spaghetti sauce business. On the downside, the spaghetti sauce is outgrossing his films.

He did graduate from Kenyon College magna cum lager and in the process begat a laundry business, which was the only student-run enterprise on Main Street. Yale University later awarded him an honorary Doctorate of Humane Letters for unknown reasons.

He has won four Sports Car Club of America national championships and is listed in the *Guinness Book of World Records* as the oldest driver (seventy) to win a professionally sanctioned race (the twenty-four-hour of Daytona, 1995).

He is married to the best actress on the planet, was number nineteen on Nixon's enemy list, and purely by accident has done fifty-one films and four Broadway plays.

He is generally considered by professionals to be the worst fisherman on the East Coast.

A. E. Hotchner has written twelve books and six plays, and in one way or another food has found its way into all of them. In *Papa Hemingway*, which was published in twenty-six languages in thirty-eight countries, there are vivid descriptions of memorable meals with Hemingway and dishes that Hemingway particularly liked. Of course, some of the dishes, like Hemingway's peanut butter on rye with a thick slice of Bermuda onion on top for breakfast, may not set you to licking your chops, but some of the other Hemingway-inspired dishes—such as the Hotch Potch (page 90)—definitely will.

Hotch has graphically described meals in some of his novels, most recently in *Louisiana Purchase*. In an earlier book, *King of the Hill*, Hotch depicted the summer of his life when he was twelve and there was no food on the table; to assuage his hunger he sometimes cut food ads from magazines and ate them. His dishes in this book demonstrate how far up the gourmet ladder he has climbed.